In order for all inhabitants to take advantage of the sun and the view of the port of Aarhus, the architects cut this ensemble into four L-shaped slabs. By giving these slabs an alternating jagged profile, even the inhabitants in the back between the other buildings can see a glimpse of the sea. In the spaciousness of the design the architects recognized the image of the iceberg, which they subsequently underlined by cladding the building with white façade panels.

Salewa Headquarters in Bolzano, Italy, by Cino Zucchi Architetti and Park Associati (2007-2011)

The Blue Planet in Copenhagen by 3XN (2013)

In the Italian Alps, along the road towards Austria, mountaineering company Salewa has built its new headquarters. The architects conceived the building as a rock crystal. The more rock-like parts of the building have been clad in colorful, perforated aluminum panels and house logistical functions. The more crystal-like parts of the building have been clad in glass and house the offices. The relatively large building forms an abstract version of the surrounding landscape, creating a harmony with it. At one of its ends the rock crystal-building has its own climbing wall.

The National Aquarium in Copenhagen lays a stone's throw away from the sea, at the landing point of the Øresund Bridge that connects Denmark with Sweden. The building has been designed by 3XN as a whirlpool that seems to almost pull people in. The chosen iconography forms a theatrical reference to the underwater world that can be explored inside and at the same time organizes the program: the various aquaria have been curled around the central round hall.

Museum for Architectural Drawing in Berlin by Speech (2009-2013)

Repetitive architectural drawings have been applied as a relief on the concrete façade. At some places the patterns overlap, like papers lying on top of each other. As the façade makes clear, this is a museum that exhibits architectural drawings. The museum was founded by one of the architects of Speech. The varying building mass is meant to underline the sketchiness of a lot of drawings.

Beijing Airport by Foster + Partners (2003-2008)

With its gentle curves, its raised flaps and streamlined edges, the roof of the largest terminal in China looks a bit like the wing of an airplane. With its form the building radiates the same technical precision and commercial efficiency as that of a design of an airplane and prepares travellers for their journey through the air.

Just before the 2008 credit crunch, 3XN designed these new headquarters for the Icelandic Landsbanki. The design is inspired by the basalt rock formations that are found throughout the island. The many large roof lights bring the low Icelandic sun into the interior, which has been left as open as possible. As a kind of rock landscape the building brings something of the outdoor lifestyle, which the Icelanders cherish, into the capital city.

Landsbanki in Reykjavik by 3XN (2007)

Mary Rose Museum in Portsmouth, UK, by Wilkinson Eyre (2008-2013)

In the Mary Rose Museum the hull of the flagship of the British King Henry VII (1491- 1547), which was found in 1982, is exhibited. The museum has been built around the remnants of the ship and displays on different floors, corresponding to the floors on the ship, what happened on a vessel like this. The exterior of the building forms an abstract version of the ship, with its own wooden hull, stern and loopholes.

According to the architects 'the fluid form of water in motion' has inspired their design of the center that houses the most important swimming and diving pools of the 2012 London Olympics. The double curved roof is shaped in such a way that both the permanent and temporary stands are provided with optimal views on the pools.

London Aquatics Centre by Zaha Hadid Architects (2005-2011)

King Abdulaziz Center of Knowledge and Culture in Saudi Arabia by Snøhetta (from 2007 onwards)

At the point where Saudi-Arabia borders the United Arab Emirates, in the desert city of Dharam, the Aramco Oil Company is building a large cultural center that houses an auditorium, a cinema, a library, an exhibition hall, a museum and an archive. Snøhetta has designed the cultural center as a collection of enlarged keystones. This way, the building strongly relates to the desert landscape and turns away from the blistering sun in very recognizable manner. In a way the design can also be considered a celebration of the land, the land that has given the area its wealth.

Il Volcano Buono in Naples by Renzo Piano Building Workshop (1995-2007)

The design by Foster + Partners for the first private spaceport, of Virgin Galactic, evokes all kinds of associations. The design has something of a ray that camouflages itself with the colors of the ground. The architecture office itself emphasizes that the design is inspired by the design of the airplanes that take the travelers into space. As a protection against the desert climate of New Mexico, the building is partially lowered into the ground.

'As a bulge in the earth's surface, a modest volcano or vulcaniello as they say in Naples', Renzo Piano describes his design for this shopping mall. With this shape, which results in a functional circular shopping circuit, the building becomes an integral part of the natural landscape, which is mentally dominated by the Vesuvius volcano. To further clarify the chosen iconography the building is fitted with a green roof.

Spaceport America in New Mexico, USA, by Foster + Partners (2006-2014)

Olympic and Paralympic Shooting Venues in London by Magma architecture (2012)

The Mosaic Park that Casanova+Hernandez has designed in Jinzhou forms a continuous surface that consists of 884 irregularly shaped pieces. At one place the park bulges up to create a small museum. The pieces of the park are filled with fragments of Chinese ceramics or with flowers.

For the 2012 London Olympics at the historic Royal Artillery Barracks, Magma has designed three temporary shooting venues. The buildings have been fitted with a double, translucent PVC skin. The skin has been fixed by a set of steel rings that have turned the (flabby) flat surfaces into (tight) double curved surfaces. The round holes that the steel rings make allow fresh air into the building. The protuberances look like enlarged bullet holes and add some drama to the sport.

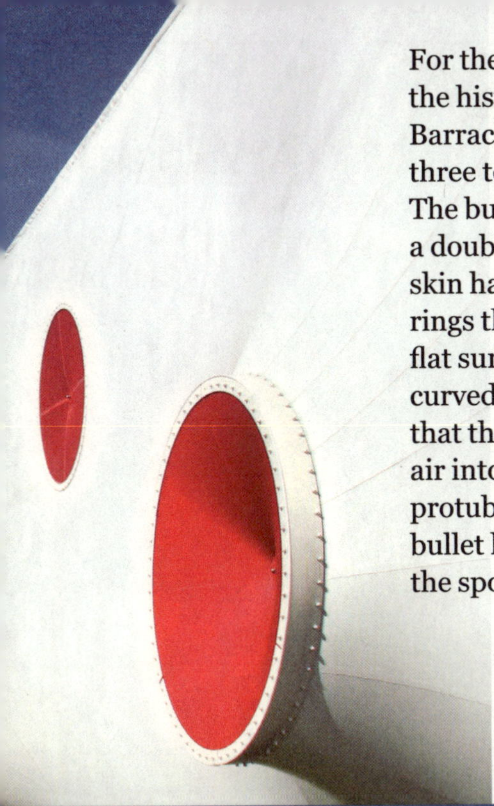

Ceramic Museum and Mosaic Park in Jinzhou by Casanova+Hernandez (2011-2013)

Oceanium of Basel Zoo by HHF and Burckhardt + Partner (2011)

In this competition entry for the design of the Oceanium of Basel Zoo the fish on display swim around in a system of grottos. The concrete dome construction makes it possible to stack the different aquaria on top of each other at this urban site. The sense of wonder that comes with a visit to a grotto, is all that a visit to the Oceanium should achieve too.

Building as

Michiel van Raaij

nai010 publishers

Ornament

Iconography in Contemporary Architecture

Contents

Preface

As a child, I grew up in a house without right angles. The house had a symmetrical, octagonal hall. All the rooms facing the hall had a different, irregular shape, sometimes with more corners and sometimes fewer. Most of the windows had the shape of an irregular pentagon. My father, who was trained as an artist, told me that he had designed the house as a crystal. In the hall, he later placed a large amethyst as a sublimation of this idea.

During my studies in architecture at the Delft University of Technology, I soon realized how growing up in such a house had shaped me. Whereas my classmates had trouble with the free-form buildings of the German architect Hans Sharoun or the American architect Daniel Libeskind, I felt immediately at home. In addition to rectangular buildings, I just as easily designed structures with extremely complex shapes. The 3D modeling software and foam cutters allowed for the various form studies, but the design teachers were more difficult. If I wanted to use angles other than the standard 90 degrees, I needed clear arguments to be able to convince them.

Especially in the first years of my study I was hesitant about taking some of my ideas about beauty seriously. For example, in the forest I imagined how branching structures could fossilize to become complex-shaped vaults. In the mountains I imagined how rock walls could form the façades of buildings. With rivers, I imagined how the collected gravel could be scaled up to create a heat-defying desert city.

Gradually, however, I discovered that my ideas were not as crazy as I initially had thought. I discovered that the Modernists had conducted extensive research into crystals and other natural structures, such as coral and air bubbles. In Art Nouveau, steel structures were derived from naturally branching structures. In an interview for the student magazine, of which I was editor-in-chief for a year, the Dutch architect Erick van Egeraat told me that he had imagined some of his buildings as rock formations. Later on, he even called one of his designs "The Rock". It turned out that the same applied to the Norwegian architectural firm Snøhetta (literally: snow mountain). Besides its more restrained work, in the desert of Saudi Arabia the firm also designed a building that has the shape of a collection of enlarged keystones that lean against each other.

In addition to these natural metaphors, in the middle of the first decade of the twenty-first century, very different types of metaphors began to emerge. The strangely shaped ING House in Amsterdam, designed by the Dutch architecture firm MVSA, became popularly known as the "clap skate". The headquarters for Swiss Re, which was designed by Foster + Partners in London, was quickly referred to as "the erotic gherkin".

For the central station in Rotterdam, British architect William Alsop designed an entryway that the media compared to champagne glasses. What did all this mean? This type of architecture could count on great public interest, but the corresponding discussions had no common ground at all with what I had learned about architecture at the university.

At the same time, I discovered design studies by the American architecture firm Asymptote in which form elements of popular products, such as sneakers, cars and mobile phones, were placed in an architectural context. The pavilion that the firm earlier had designed for the Floriade exhibition in Hoofddorp included elements of an airplane: a streamlined, symmetrical steel body with canopies like wings. According to the architects, this was a reference to the nearby Schiphol airport, which dominates the region.

Soon thereafter, I read an essay by the Spanish-British architect Alejandro Zearo-Polo in which he explained how an architect can use a metaphor for two purposes: to structure the function and organization of the building and to sell the design to the client and the general public. This taught me that the public's experience of a building and the architect's design can correspond. Moreover, this design approach can produce an architecture in which the façade really tells something about the function of the building and how it is organized, potentially a very specific and eloquent architecture. A whole new world opened up for me.

To explore this phenomenon – how are designs interpreted by the public and how do architects design buildings with this in mind? – I mapped it out in more detail using a weblog. Over several years I collected around 150 examples of buildings, which in the eyes of the public or their designer were also something else: a cloud, a hat or a letter from the alphabet. The examples I found were sometimes more literal and sometimes more abstract. Sometimes they also explained the function, the organization or the context of the building, but sometimes they did not. It was only the tip of the iceberg.

While more and more evidence accumulated, it turned out that surprisingly little had been written about the use of metaphors in architecture. Architects that use metaphors in their work, such as the Dutch landscape architect Adriaan Geuze or the American architect Steven Holl, spoke about these metaphors in their lectures, but they avoided the topic in the books about their work. It almost seemed that they were embarrassed about their approach. But hadn't it been more than a century since the Austrian architect Adolf Loos had forbidden ornament in architecture? Moreover, wasn't the current era incomparable with that in which Loos worked?

Due to the lack of theory, the debate on this phenomenon developed very slowly. Both the popularity and criticism of the "icons" expanded. The formalistic buildings that were being realized all over the world were often found to be too costly and impractical. It rarely came to a constructive debate about the cultural value that this architecture represented too. What was lacking, what is still lacking, is a theoretical framework with which the quality of the designs can be assessed.

I decided that if architects do not write about this themselves I would simply interview them about their ideas on this topic – that idea is the foundation of this book. Supported by nai010 publishers, I found eight architects and two architectural historians who were willing to speak out on this topic. The various interviews complement each other, sometimes overlap briefly and sometimes contradict each other. Combined, they form a coherent theory about the use of metaphors in architecture.

However, this is not a comprehensive scientific study. It is not intended as such. I hope that this book will provide the debate about the use of metaphors with more substantive depth and that it will provide substantive support to architects in designing buildings as ornaments. Finally, I hope that the book will lead to subsequent studies on this topic. It is a starting point.

Enjoy!

Introduction

Herning Museum of Contemporary Art in Herning, Denmark, by Steven Holl Architects (2005)

TABACCHI

Characteristic images from outside architecture that are used in architecture to explain the nature of the building. In a nutshell, that is what the use of iconography in contemporary architecture is about. That is the building as ornament.

A rock formation, a letter of the alphabet, a dress, an airplane – as long as the image explains the character of the building, hardly any limits are imposed on the themes of the images that are used.

The chosen theme is often derived from the function of the building. For instance, a car museum can be designed with rounded shapes, continuous windows and a metallic skin. The primary shape of an ambassador's residence can be reminiscent of the national flag of his or her country. An aquarium can take the form of a huge water vortex that "pulls" visitors inside.

Besides the function of the building, its context is often used as a theme as well. A park in the capital may refer to an important landscape elsewhere in the country. A library built on a rocky background can take the shape of enlarged boulders. A hotel that is built in the water can tell nautical stories with a shape that refers to a wind-filled sail.

The function and context may also coincide thematically. A school building near a port, in which students are trained to work in the port, that elicits images of industrial port facilities and stacked shipping containers, can explain both its function and context. The same applies to an art museum founded by textile magnates next to an old textile factory, where textiles also play an important role in the exhibited art. By choosing textile as a theme in the architecture, both the function and the context of the museum can be explained.

These examples show that the function and context of a building can be interpreted in many ways. Regarding its function, a characteristic component can be enlarged. Regarding its context, a characteristic component can also be taken from the broader context.

In some cases the function and/or context can be explained with a humorous or ironic reference. An example would be a police station with windows like bullet holes. Ultimately, even political messages are possible. For example, a museum whose collection is of dubious origin can be given a shaky-looking composition.

As long as the client and the public experience the chosen theme as a virtue and the iconography explains the nature of the building, the possibilities are basically endless.

From Different Angles

At the end of the 1980s and in the early 1990s, the use of iconography in architecture emerged simultaneously in many places. From 1984 through 1988, Steven Holl Architects worked on a house in Martha's Vineyard that incorporated the image of whale ribs. It is located near the whale skeleton described in the novel *Moby Dick* that was used as the frame for a house. From 1989 through 1994, Herzog & de Meuron worked on the Signal Box in Basel: a building to accommodate machinery with the appearance of an abstracted spool.

From 1991 through 1997, West 8 in Rotterdam worked on the Schouwburgplein, in which elements of the port were represented. From 1994 through 1997, Neutelings Riedijk Architects worked on the design of the Minnaert Building, a geology faculty in which images of the earth and a cave were incorporated. From 1995 through 2004, Foreign Office Architects worked on the Yokohama International Port Terminal, a building that is organized as a set of waves on water.

What is the origin of this approach to architecture?

Due to the very diverse backgrounds of the various architecture offices, a common source of inspiration, in the form of a single key project or spiritual father, can be ruled out. At the end of the 1980s and early 1990s, a cultural-economic movement gained momentum in which architecture was given more freedom. The roots of the architecture that emerged go deep into architectural history.

Figurative Sculpture and the Theory of Character

One of the basic themes of architecture is the sometimes very literal representation of something outside architecture. The origin of this theme lies in the transformation of figurative sculpture into architecture and the development of the theory of character.

Shipping and Transport College in Rotterdam by Neutelings Riedijk Architects (2001-2006)

In classical antiquity, and even before, figurative sculpture was a standard component of architecture. Freestanding sculptures could be found in, on and behind the façade. Flattened sculptures could be seen in friezes, in temple fronts and in tableaux. In this type of sculpture, stories were told that were related to the function of the building.

The first transformation of these figurative sculptures into architecture could have been the Caryatids and Atlantes: the female and male figures that were used as columns in ancient Greece. No further transformation of sculpture into building took place for centuries.

'In later centuries, architects repeatedly saw opportunities during the transitions between various styles,' states the Dutch architecture historian Bernard Colenbrander. In these interim periods, architects saw possibilities to build bridges between figurative sculpture and archi-

Façade of the cemetery of Chaux, France, by Claude-Nicolas Ledoux (1804)

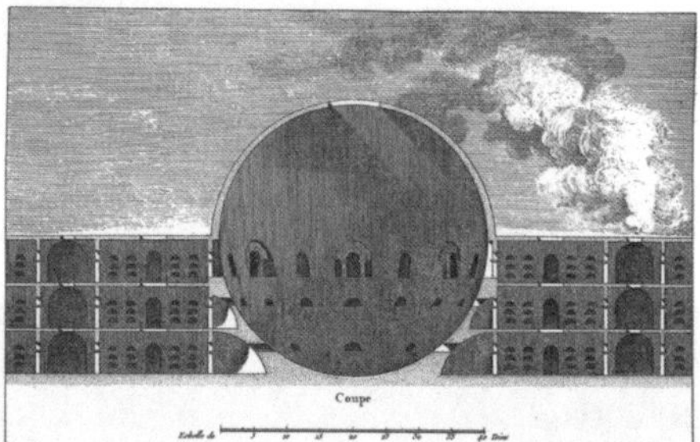

Brothel of Chaux, France, by Claude-Nicolas Ledoux (1804)

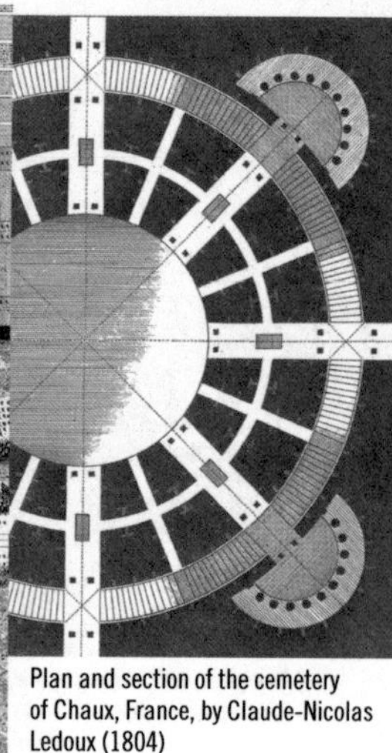

Plan and section of the cemetery of Chaux, France, by Claude-Nicolas Ledoux (1804)

tecture; they sought the limits of their profession – and sometimes exceeded them.

The first of these interim periods occurred around the time of the French Revolution (1789-1799). Several decades before this, the French architect Claude Nicolas Ledoux (1736-1806) had defined the principles of *Architecture Parlante*: architecture should explain its own function and identity. To this end, Ledoux used legible building masses, compiled from elementary volumes. He had no difficulty deviating from the schematics of classical antiquity and looking beyond the traditional borders of architecture.

In 1804, as the most radical illustration of his ideas, Ledoux designed the ideal city of Chaux – which was never built. For the city, he designed a bordello with a floor plan in the shape of an erect phallus. For the cemetery in the city, Ledoux designed a building around a perfectly spherical space that cannot be entered – you can only see into it from a number of points. According to Ledoux, this space could represent both absolute emptiness and the universe: the earth in relation to the planets. To express the character of a building, Ledoux believed that it was sometimes much more satisfactory to scale up figurative sculpture to architecture than to continue using the schematics from classical antiquity.

Contemporaries of Ledoux, such as Jean Jacques Lequeu (1757-1826), designed comparable projects. 'For example, Lequeu designed buildings in the form of animals, such as a cow,' explains Colenbrander. After the French Revolution, in 1813, Napoleon Bonaparte commissioned a twelve meter high watchtower at the Place de la Bastille in the shape of an elephant – to illustrate his own resolution. Architect Jean-Antoine Alavoine (1778-1834) designed the structure in copper, but due to lack of funding it was implemented in wood and plaster. In 1846 the

Elephant of Bastille in Paris by Jean-Antoine Alavoine (1813)

dilapidated watchtower was demolished.

'Not coincidentally, the designs of Ledoux and Lequeu were created in the same period that the first picturesque gardens were designed, which included follies,' relates Colenbrander. These gardens played with perspectives. The follies could also take on all kinds of shapes, such as newly built ruins. 'The follies escaped from the conventions of classicism and Gothic architecture. Moreover, they were always figurative and were intended to stimulate the senses.'

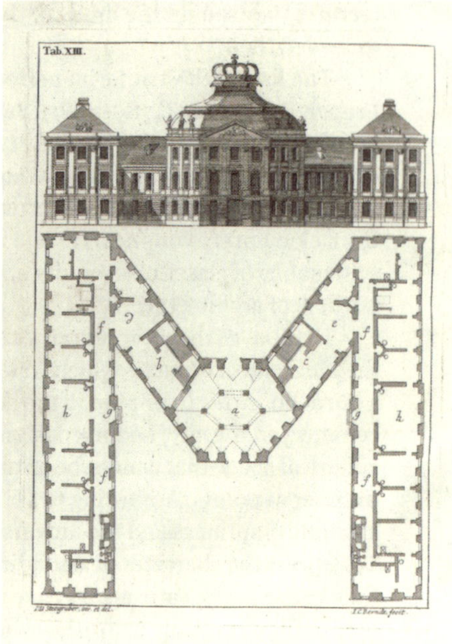

Letter M by Johann David Steingruber (1773)

Also worth mentioning in this context is the architectural alphabet that the German architect Johann David Steingruber (1702-1787) designed in 1773. For each letter in the alphabet, Steingruber drew a building whose floor plan had the shape of that letter. He also imagined a suitable function and façade for each letter.

The theory of character that was introduced with the *Architecture Parlante* was developed further in the nineteenth century. Every building was to be given a character suitable for its function and status in society. For example, in its general composition and ornamentation, a City Hall should tell a story about the function that it fulfills. Moreover, to emphasize its higher status in society, a City Hall should be decorated much more richly than for instance a house.

Entrance of metro station Porte Dauphine in Paris by Hector Guimard (1900)

In contrast to the designs of Ledoux and Lequeu, in the nineteenth century, the character of a building was designed with strictly architectural means. Jack was back in the box. 'Architecture became much more abstract,' admits Colenbrander. 'But the figurative was never far away.' Certainly at the end of the nineteenth century, the sculpture and tableaux in the façades of buildings became increasingly free once again. Coinciding with this, the figures based on Greek and Roman antiquity were gradually replaced by contemporary variants.

For several years around the turn of the century, the "whiplash" and plant motifs in Art Nouveau were given a prominent place in architecture. In the tradition of the follies, architect Hector Guimard (1867-1942) designed a series of entrances for the Paris Metro for which the plant motif, and nothing else, gave shape to the architecture. Sculpture and architecture had fused together. In his design, Guimard celebrated the structural efficiency of the world of plants. The ornament didn't explain the function or the context of the entrances though.

In the architecture of the nineteenth century and early twentieth century, and even in the Art Nouveau, Guimard's design is an exception. As a rule, the figurative elements retained their traditional, subsidiary role in the design and did not yet influence the architectural composition as a whole.

The Jump in Scale

All this changed during the next interim period in architecture: the beginning of Modernism. In early Modernism, images from outside architecture – abstracted – were used for the first time on the scale of the building as a whole, and in some cases were even used to explain its character.

In his influential book *Towards an Architecture* from 1923, Le Corbusier (1887-1965) extensively discussed the design of automobiles, steam ships, airplanes and machinery. With these industrial designs, Le Corbusier wanted to show which language of form emerged from functionality and mass production. In his own work, the references to these objects from outside architecture usually remained abstract. He focused on their underlying principles. However, many of his contemporaries translated the metaphors used by Le Corbusier and others more literally into architecture.

For example, many functionalistic buildings from this era have the appearance of machines. Every element of the building has been given its own shape, attuned to its function: a staircase is a cylinder, a house is a box, a theater is a wedge, and so forth. Some architects went even further. For example, in 1929 in the port city of San Sebastián, the Spanish architects Joaquín Labayen and José Manuel Aizpurúa designed a building in the shape of a steam ship, including portholes "below decks" and a panorama window around the "bridge".

In the 1930s, a new group of architects went even further as part of a movement that is now called *Streamline Moderne*. Inspired by the streamlined shape of automobiles, boats and aircrafts, they designed a series of streamlined buildings. References to boats in particular were frequently used. For example, in 1939 the American architect Robert Derrah (1895-1946) designed the Coca-Cola building in Los Angeles in the shape of an ocean liner.

In the search for a new visual language for architecture, images from outside architecture were woven into architecture. In the rejection of ornament on a small scale, ornament on the scale of the entire building was introduced, albeit unintentionally.

According to Colenbrander, after this interim period, the literal translation of such metaphors was soon a thing of the past. 'It was immediately codified again.' Consequently, architecture was once again nothing other than architecture.

In the interim period itself, the theme of the ornament, used at the scale of the building as a whole, was often generic. A relationship between the function and context of the building and the image woven into the architecture only occasionally was found. For example, the "steam ship" of Labayen and Aizpurúa was home to the Real Club Náutico in the port of San Sebastián. Consequently, this metaphor explained both the function and the context of the building. However, with the Coca-Cola Building, this wasn't the case at all. Behind the portals of this building, soft drinks were being manufactured. The image of the ocean liner primarily expressed the belief in progress.

The link between the transformation of sculpture into architecture, which was completed at the beginning of the twentieth century, and the theory of character from the nineteenth century became definitive only in the 1970s with the publication of the book *Learning from Las Vegas* (1972) by the American architects Robert Venturi, Denise Scott Brown and Steven Izenour, and the book *The Language of Post-Modern Architecture* (1977) by the British architectural historian Charles Jencks. It was especially the Duck concept of Venturi and Scott Brown – a building that portrays its function with its figurative form – that definitively opened the door for the emergence of the building as ornament.

El Real Club Nautique in San Sebasián, Spain, by Joaquín Labayen en José Manuel Aizpurúa (1929)

Liberation

As stated above, the building as ornament emerged at multiple locations simultaneously at the end of the 1980s and early 1990s. In Switzerland, Herzog & de Meuron used the new materials – with which they had been experimenting for some time – no longer to articulate building components, but to enable the building itself to "speak" as a three-dimensional object. In the United States, Steven Holl began using metaphors more emphatically to structure his designs, instead of merely to give shape to them. In the Netherlands, the Office for Metropolitan Architecture (OMA) became a training ground for a group of architects who would later on all begin to design ornamental buildings in their own way.

'In the 1980s, it was impossible to talk with Rem Koolhaas about the material codes of the architectural profession,' says Colenbrander, who closely followed OMA at that time. 'Koolhaas had two role models, Frank Lloyd Wright and Walter Gropius, but these role models were not expressed in architecture. In his view, the architectural profession was a mentality. And this mentality was dominated by hauteur – hence Wright – and by the willingness to take advantage of group work –

Coca-Cola Building in Los Angeles by Robert Derrah (1939)

hence Gropius. From that mentality, you could rethink the world. That was the ambition of Koolhaas.'

'At OMA, the architects worked without architectural references. At most, there were picturesque references. Not without reason did Madelon Vriesendorp, Koolhaas' wife, make paintings at OMA that stood completely independent from architecture. These were picturesque paintings,' concludes Colenbrander. In 1995, he wrote the book *Referentie OMA* about the generation of architects that had learned their profession at OMA and built on that in their own practices. 'These architects were no longer connected to a common architectural code. For them, the architectural profession had become a mental affair.'

Bjarke Ingels (BIG), Winy Maas (MVRDV) and Alejandro Zaero-Polo (formerly Foreign Office Architects, now AZPML), whose work is discussed extensively in this book, all worked at OMA at some point. This was also the case for Willem-Jan Neutelings, the partner of Michiel Riedijk (Neutelings Riedijk Architects). According to Colenbrander, at OMA the architects learned to make designs that were free from architectural traditions. 'It was a *tabula rasa*: there was nothing on the paper that they started with.'

According to Colenbrander this explains why these architecture offices began to include images from outside architecture in their work at the end of the 1980s and early 1990s. In his rejection of every architectural tradition, Koolhaas enabled a figurative tradition to emerge. This is illustrated by the many sketch models that were made from blue foam at OMA. These small models no longer suggested architectural structures. They were figures.

Whereas Koolhaas himself tries to reverse every convention and

Guggenheim Museum in Bilbao by Gehry Partners (1993-1997)

has a strong predilection for elusive forms, the architects who have learned their profession at his firm use a different approach. Liberated from architectural traditions, they feel free to use ornament at the scale of the building.

With OMA, Koolhaas essentially forced a third interim period into existence. This was an interim period that also emerged at other places and for the first time in architectural history appears to be permanent.

The Market

In various ways, the late 1980s and early 1990s formed a turning point. Postmodernism, the movement that should have followed Modernism, appeared to have no support outside of a small group of enthusiasts and was rejected by the new generation of architects. In 1988, the Museum of Modern Art (MoMA) held an architecture exhibition in New York with the title Deconstructivism. This could hardly be called a movement either, but it did indicate that architecture was already moving in a subsequent direction. In short, this was a time when the old models stalled, but a new recipe had not yet clearly emerged.

That moment of artistic freedom coincided with the unprecedented optimism that was the result of the fall of the Berlin wall in 1989. That is to say: optimism about the market. Certainly in Europe, the government-driven society was rapidly being replaced by a world in which the market provided everything.

According to Colenbrander, the emergence of market thinking has caused a radical reversal in the relationship between the client and the architect. 'On the market, everyone is right – in principle,' explains Colenbrander. 'If a client wants to pay for something, he should get it. The customer is always right.' This assertive client no longer believes the architect at his word. In this new context, says Colenbrander, the authority previously enjoyed by the architect quickly erodes. The architect now has to sell his design to the client.

'The new relationship between client and architect makes architecture accessible, by definition, to other sources of inspiration. The difference between high culture and low culture has disappeared. A house can look like a traditional house or like an animal. Anything is possible.'

With the emergence of market thinking, the old criteria used to assess buildings also cease to apply. From now on, designs are primarily evaluated for their public appeal and their commercial success. A new type of iron logic emerges: the more visitors attracted by a design, the better it is.

The Catalyst

In terms of success, the Guggenheim Museum designed by the American architect Frank Gehry in Bilbao (1993-1997) is unequaled. Since its opening, the museum has drawn around 1 million visitors per year. The architecture of the museum certainly contributed to this success.

The success of the Guggenheim Museum in Bilbao gave enormous momentum to the concept of the building as ornament. Although few architects know that the Guggenheim is a building as an ornament, there was no other way to design it besides conceiving the building in this way.

How did Gehry himself arrive at his design? In an interview with Thomas Pritzker, Gehry explained the development of his work as follows:

'I let the forms be the thing. I wanted [. . .] to get passion and feeling into the building without resorting to nineteenth century models. I thought of movement, because we live in an age of movement. My precedents for this go back to sculptor Phidias at the Parthenon, who was able to convey a sense of movement with the shields of the warriors pushing into the stone. When you see it in the British Museum, you feel the pressure. And then the Shiva, the dancing figures. You look at them, look back, and you're sure they'd moved. That was my inspiration, and I thought: can we do it at this big scale?

And there are some fish stories that go along with it. When the Postmodern stuff happened, when my colleagues went back to Greek temples, I got pissed off and said: If you go back, why don't you go back three million years before men, to fish? I started drawing fish and it started to have a life of its own. It became fish lamps, and other things. I started to look at the carp and the Koi fish in the pond, and they are very architectural. And I started to explore those shapes. I made a terrible one, a thirty-five foot wooden fish for a fashion company at Pity Palace in Florence. It was super kitsch. But it had that sense of movement. And everybody got it. And then I tried to cut off the tail, cut off the head, cut of the fins, start to abstract it, and start to look how far I could go before I lost it. I did a room for the Walker Art Museum, and I did a thing for Chiat Day. From that I learned to build with those forms and capture that kind of feeling. That was the evolution.'

The remarkable visual language of the Guggenheim Museum in the former industrial city of Bilbao illustrates in particular the special status of the building in the city, even in the world. It is a building with a unique character. The image of the fish, in this case a school of fish, however does not explain the function of the building.

In the decade following the completion of the Museum, almost every architect was asked at some point by a client to design buildings that would appeal in a comparable fashion to a broad public, and would put their company or city "on the map". Not every architect who was asked this question was also prepared to question his own approach to architecture. However, the architects who did begin to look for a new approach in many cases ended up with the building as ornament. The route that they took to reach this point was very personal and differed greatly between architects.

How widely spread this design method has become, is illustrated by the fact that every architect uses a different vocabulary to describe his work: idea, duck, ornament, icon, iconography, "manimal", advertisement . . . . These are all different words for the same concept: the building as ornament.

Swiss Re Headquarters in London by Foster + Partners (1997-2004)

World Financial Centre in Shanghai by KPF (1997-2008)

The Cloud in Seoul by MVRDV (2011)

ING House in Amsterdam by MVSA (1998-2002)

Reading and Writing

At the end of the 1980s and the beginning of the 1990s, the newly acquired cultural freedom and the emergence of market thinking coincided with the introduction of the first computers in the design process. This made it much simpler for architects to design buildings with complex shapes. For example, the design of the Guggenheim Museum in Bilbao could not have been realized so quickly if Gehry had not been able to design it in 3D on the computer.

Although computer design technology was not a prerequisite for the emergence of the building as ornament, the development of this technology has accelerated this process. The media in which architects work – manual sketches, models, drawing software – partly determine their way of thinking, and thus what kind of designs they make.

This newly attained freedom quickly led to a wide variety of new shapes for buildings. To identify these shapes, the public likes to compare them with what it knows. Norman Foster designed the Swiss Re office in downtown London as an elongated egg. The building however reminded the public particularly of a penis or a pickle. In popular parlance it was therefore quickly called "the erotic gherkin".

Several years before, a new office building was completed for ING along the ring road of Amsterdam. According to the Dutch architecture firm MVSA, the aerodynamic shape of the building was a reference to the shapes of the passing cars and to the airplanes taking off from nearby Schiphol airport. However, the general public still compares the building to a shoe or a clap skate.

When ING later sponsored the Amsterdam Marathon, the building was provided with massive shoe laces as a joke. In this way, the rather unfortunate association of the bank building with a shoe was cleverly converted into a virtue. Perhaps the Swiss Re tower in London one day can become the biggest "rugby ball" in Great Britain?

When architects do not sufficiently consider the associations that buildings can evoke with the general public, this can lead to unwelcome surprises. Whereas the associations evoked by the Swiss Re tower and the ING House can still be referred to as "awkward", the American architecture firm Kohn Pederson Fox (KPF) evoked an extremely negative association with its original design for the World Financial Center (WFC) in Shanghai. In the top of the tower – one of the tallest buildings in the world – the original design called for a large round hole. However, the building was being developed by the Japanese company Mori. With the Japanese occupation of China during World War II in mind, the Chinese authorities saw the round hole as a depiction of the Japanese flag. This went down the wrong way. The authorities blocked the construction until the round hole was replaced by a parallelogram.

While the discussion about the design by KPF took place behind the scenes, this can also occur via the media in the public eye. This happened to the Dutch architecture firm MVRDV when it published its design for a residential building in a new high-rise district in Seoul. The firm had designed two residential towers that were connected in the middle by a pixelated cloud with shared facilities. Immediately after the presentation of the design, fierce criticism appeared on various websites. Americans in particular, saw the design as a representation of the attacks on the World Trade Center in New York. This led to furious reactions, and even threats to MVRDV. National media throughout the world reported on the controversy. One day after the presentation of the design, the firm published a statement in which it offered its excuses for the association that the design had evoked: these associations were not intended. During the design process, the firm had not noticed the similarity with images of the WTC attacks.

In his book *The Architecture of Happiness* (2006) the British philosopher Alain de Botton states that architecture should portray virtues.

Bird's Nest Stadium in Beijing by Herzog & de Meuron with Ai Weiwei (2002-2008)

Yokohama International Port Terminal, Japan, by Foreign Office Architects (1995-200)

No architect wishes to design buildings that evoke improper associations. It was therefore only a matter of time before architects would begin to purposefully direct the associations evoked by their freeform buildings.

While the above-mentioned architecture firms first had to make mistakes before they could really begin to seriously account for such associations in their design process, other firms immediately discovered the benefits of including a desired association in their designs.

The British architectural firm Foreign Office Architects discovered the substantial benefits of a precise association when they presented their design for the Yokohama International Port Terminal in Japan. During the public presentation, architect Alejandro Zaero-Polo noted that his traditional explanation of the design was not coming across. However, the design had also been informed, behind the scenes, by the iconography of the wave. When he explained that idea, he saw that the public immediately understood the design: it was a wave! Consequently, he discovered that as an architect he could use iconography to "sell" his design to clients, the public and the media. Certainly for public buildings, this turned out to be a formula for success.

Inside the Bird's Nest Stadium

Free forms that evoke associations, and directing these associations by using an image from outside architecture in architectural design; that is the basis for the building as ornament. No event illustrated the power of this architecture better than the 2008 Olympic Games in Beijing. The Bird's Nest Stadium, designed by the Swiss architectural firm Herzog & de Meuron, and the Aquatic Center, designed by the Australian firm PTW, were publicized worldwide in the national media. These were recognizable and unique shapes with only virtuous references, which in the case of the Aquatic Center clarified the function of the building too.

Definitions

The definition for ornament used in this book is derived from the theory of character that was developed in the eighteenth and nineteenth centuries and reads as follows:

> The ornament is an explanation of the function, social status, organization, load-bearing structure and/or context of the building.

There are different ways in which this explanation can take place. For example, there is direct representation, in which the spatial organization of a building is made visible in its mass structure. But there is also exaggeration, in which a construction detail for instance is enlarged to demonstrate how the load-bearing structure works.

The explanation on which this book focuses is iconography, which is in the context of architecture is defined as follows:

> Iconography is the use of images from outside architecture in architecture.

This book focuses specifically on iconography as an explanation, although iconography as such does not necessarily has to explain anything. A building that is interpreted by the public as iconographic, but that has not been designed as such by the architect, has a non-explaining iconography. The Swiss Re tower is an example of such an iconographic building.

This stands in contrast to an iconography that explains the function, social status, organization, load-bearing structure and/or context of the building. It is this iconography that is advocated in this book. An iconography can explain one of the above-mentioned aspects, for example the function of the building. But an iconography can also explain multiple aspects simultaneously, for example the function, organization and load-bearing structure. For that matter, the explanation of the function and/or context of the building occurs most frequently in practice.

In this book, ornament is linked to iconography. An ornament is not iconographic by definition. If a console is enlarged during its implementation to clarify its function or is differentiated in terms of the materials used, it can be called ornamental. If the console is provided with a curl, plant motif or human figure, it can also be referred to as iconographic.

In this book, the concepts of ornament and iconography are used interchangeably. The term ornament is used as an umbrella concept, while iconography is its concrete implementation.

The title of this book, *Building as Ornament*, following the definition above simply indicates explanations at the scale of the building as a whole. As a concept, it is broader than the application of iconography alone. However, to put force behind the argument in this book, “the building as ornament” is here frequently used as a synonym for the use of iconography. Although this is not entirely correct, it does have two important advantages. In this way, the concept of ornament is detached from the concept of decoration and directly linked with something entirely different: iconography. Even more important is that the concept of iconography is thus detached from the generic concept of the icon, and due to the link to ornamentation, is placed in a historical perspective. In this way iconography can also be linked directly to the ambition of the ornament: to explain. The use of iconography does not lead to banal image architecture, as some architects and critics claim, but results in deliberate, eloquent architecture.

In art history, the word iconography (literally: writing with images) is an extension of the word icon. Architectural historian Charles Jencks and architect Michiel Riedijk still refer to a building in which iconography is used as an icon. However, during the past two decades the word icon has acquired a much broader meaning due to its intensive use. The word icon now usually refers to a landmark building in the city: a contemporary monument. This does not necessarily mean that iconography has been used. The concepts of icon and iconography should therefore be used separately. To prevent confusion, the word icon has been avoided wherever possible in this book. Instead, the word iconography is linked to the building as ornament.

Ten Interviews

This book contains ten interviews on the use of iconography in contemporary architecture. In order of appearance, the speakers are architectural historians Auke van der Woud and Charles Jencks, and the architects Denise Scott Brown, Adriaan Geuze, Michiel Riedijk, Alejandro Zaero-Polo, Ben van Berkel, Steven Holl, Winy Maas and Bjarke Ingels.

From the various interviews, a picture emerges of a field that is defined by three poles: iconographic detail, layered iconography and singular iconography. The architects interviewed each occupy a unique place in relation to these three poles.

Adriaan Geuze and Michiel Riedijk, each in their own way, focus on nineteenth century ornamentation. Besides the emphasis on a recognizable silhouette, the iconography in their work is primarily contained in the architectural detail. Ben van Berkel, Alejandro Zaero and Steven Holl focus on a layered iconography that cannot be immediately understood, but gradually reveals itself during repeated visits to the building. Winy Maas and Bjarke Ingels focus on the clearest possible communication with a singular iconography.

To relate the various interviews to each other as much as possible, the three approaches distinguished above are clustered in this book. Starting from architectural history, the iconographic detail that is rooted in history is discussed first, followed by the layered iconography and then the singular iconography.

Rockmagneten in Roskilde, Denmark, by MVRDV and COBE (2011)

Watercube in Beijing by PTW Architects and Arup (2008)

Interview Auke van der Woud

The Aquarium of Artis Zoo in Amsterdam by Gerlof Salm and Abraham Salm (1879-1980)

'An ornament provides specific details of expression and explains them'

Auke van der Woud (1947) is emeritus professor of architecture and history of urban architecture at the University of Groningen. Van der Woud has specialized in the development of Dutch architecture, urban design and landscape architecture in the 19th century. He has presented his research in the books *Het lege land* (1987), *Waarheid en karakter* (1997) and *Een nieuwe wereld* (2006). In 2010, he received the Rotterdam Maaskant Prize in recognition of his work.

To begin with, what is your definition of ornament, and how does ornament differ from decoration? Partly due to the writings of architect Adolf Loos, these two concepts have become virtually synonymous in contemporary language.

'If you look at these concepts from the nineteenth century perspective, decoration and ornament are not the same. Decoration is that which makes something beautiful, such as a fresco, curtains or paneling. Or a marble floor, in the case of the architecture of Adolf Loos. This is all decoration. An ornament is something different, something more specific. An ornament provides specific details of expression and explains them.

Here in Groningen, we have the Korenbeurs, which now contains a supermarket. The rear of the building has an apse. From the outside, cast iron rosettes are visible on the wall. These rosettes are attached to the tie rods that are required for the loadbearing structure. The rosettes could have been omitted, but they weren't. In 1865 the city architect Johannes van Beusenkom considered them to be important elements and wanted them to be seen.'

So this is not decoration that can be omitted?

'No, these are important elements and they must therefore be present in all their components. These elements deserve an ornament. If something is more important, it can also cost more, it must cost more. This is based on extensive functional reasoning.'

Does the ornament also explain the function of the building?

'Yes, it does that too . . . .'

Or does it primarily concern the explanation of the loadbearing structure?

'Indeed, there is a strong relationship between the ornament and the loadbearing structure. This has a long tradition. If a beam ends at a wall, a console is designed to go under it. This console makes the loadbearing quality visible. In terms of structure, it is perhaps completely unnecessary, but the console can show that you are making the transition from narrow to broad, from horizontal to vertical. This is the function of an ornament; it is not to make the structure more beautiful, although it does that as well. In the first place, it is to show what the structure does, how it works.

This element was already present in Gothic architecture. If you make a transition from the surface of the wall to the glass of the window, then that happens indirectly by means of ridges, beads and other types of ornamentation. This covers the space between the wall and the glass, which is often as much as 80 cm. Of course, the transition can be made directly, but in this case it is the intention of the architect to make the transition clearer to the observer. It is all about the relation between inside and outside. In the nineteenth century, architects needed an ornament for this.

At some point, however, Adolf Loos said: do away with it. Can't one simply make this transition in a single step? The transition between beam and wall, between wall and window. Loos solved this problem in his own way. Something always has to remain visible. And that is what you see in Adolf Loos' architecture.'

The buildings designed by Adolf Loos are modest, but are also characterized by all kinds of details. It is very clever how he does that.

'Yes, Loos is unique because he understood that around 1900 ornament had been completely overused. With the emergence of the construction industry in the 1890s, for example, one could essentially purchase ornament in a store.'

In the last years of the nineteenth century, some buildings were completely covered with ornament. The Victoria Hotel in Amsterdam, opposite the Central Station, is one of the most heavily ornamented buildings in the city. Even though it is just a hotel.

'There could only be one answer to that, and that was: do away with it. The ornament became a victim of its own success, it had to go. And now it's coming back.'

I would like to return for a moment to a question that we passed by rather quickly. In their book Learning from Las Vegas *(1972), architects Robert Venturi and Denise Scott Brown linked the function of the building directly to a corresponding figurative ornament. Although they are opposed to Modernism, their thinking is based on it. The function of the building, in a narrow sense, remained for them the basis for its expression. What was the situation in this regard in the nineteenth century? Did a building with a specific function, such as a post office, have its own ornament?*

'No.'

There wasn't a kind of catalog for such ornaments?

'No. However, in 1860, the eclectic architect Willem Rose attempted to write a manual on this topic. At that time he wrote the book *De Leer van het Ornament*. It is actually a kind of thesaurus of ornaments, with ornaments from Greece, from the Baroque period, but also ornaments that he had devised himself. Although it may appear otherwise, the examples were never intended to be taken literally. His idea was that ornament must be redesigned continuously, and very precisely, by the architect. It is not a standard formula.'

In your books, you link ornament in the nineteenth century to the character of the building. How was that character designed?

'The nineteenth century was actually a continuous quest. The larger context for this quest was the discussion about style. "In which style are we building?", to paraphrase Heinrich Hübsch. The arts — and architecture was part of the arts — should express the *zeitgeist*. After religion, the arts were the highest form of cultural expression, and in the hierarchy of the arts, architecture took the highest position, because that was the most public art form.

So how was character designed? After 1860, when building projects began to be commissioned in the Netherlands (before this time the country was simply too poor), immediately a schism occurred between architects. On one side there were architects who stated that a good theoretical concept of style was still necessary. These were architects who focused on reinterpreting the Dutch Renaissance and the Gothic era. On the other side there were the architects who said: "But there is such a thing as artistic freedom. I can do what I want." These were the architects who embraced Eclecticism. What you see is that the group who focused on the theoretical concept of style, dealt very differently with character than the group of eclectics. While the first group approached design dogmatically, the second group began a creative search for the correct character, the correct ornament. It goes without saying that this took place by trial and error.

One example is the Aquarium, designed by the eclectic architect Abraham Salm together with his father in Amsterdam. Now a terribly neglected building, it also accommodates a zoological museum. To express that status, Salm designed the building with a temple façade. But this was 1879, so there was a touch of irony. It is an intelligent design. But he is also boasting: look at the amazing sights I observed during my extensive travels. This is intended for his peers, to show them his sophistication. A good architect always works on two levels: he gives the public a beautiful building, but he also shows his peers a thing or two.

Whereas eclectics such as Salm in the first place focused on their client and the public, the architects that based their work on a theoretical concept of style followed their own agenda. The group associated with the architect Pierre Cuypers preferred to design every building in neo-Gothic style, even non-religious buildings. They were fixated on that style concept. With respect to the character of the buildings, time and time again they lost their way. For example, with the Central Station in Amsterdam, you see that Cuypers had a great deal of difficulty expressing the character properly. Today, people experience this as an impressive building, because there is so much to

Victoria Hotel in Amsterdam by Johann Friedrich Henkenhaf (1889-1890)

Amsterdam Centraal Station by Pierre Cuypers (1881-1889)

De Nederlandse Bank in Amsterdam by Willem Froger (1865-1869

Faculty of Chemistry, now Faculty of Architecture, in Delft, the Netherlands, by Gerard Drecht (1918-1923)

see. But it is more Disney than majestic architecture. From a nineteenth-century perspective, it is actually an idiotic railway station building. Try comparing it to the Central Station in Antwerp. That is truly and undoubtedly a station. It has the scale that you expect from a railway station building, the proper ornament and a magnificent central hall.

Character is actually expression: expression of the function of the building, but also of its social status. For example, in the nineteenth century a bank building was hugely important. In the Spuistraat in Amsterdam, for example, such a building was completed around 1900. It is clad with granite and equipped with barred windows. This was all to show how important the building was socially. Today, this is completely different. A bank now is essentially no more important than a department store.'

There are architects who complain that today all buildings are designed in such a way that they appear to be equally important.

'In the nineteenth century, there was a strict hierarchy, and social control was of course much stronger. If you acted above your position in society, you were immediately reprimanded. If a building did not have a social function, it was not permitted to look like it had one. The other way around, it worked exactly the same. If a building was important, but did not have an important face, that was also impossible. This has everything to do with character.

For example, consider the building that architect Willem Froger designed for *De Nederlandse Bank* on the Oude Turfmarkt in Amsterdam. Criticism at the time was fierce. The building did have a long façade on the street, but it was constructed from cheap materials and had little in the way of ornamentation. This architecture was not compatible with the function of the building as the central bank of the Netherlands.

The same applied at the time to educational buildings. For example, consider the building that now accommodates the Faculty of Architecture of the TU Delft. This was designed in 1920 for the chemistry faculty. Look how detailed it is. The architect pulled out all the stops. Why? Because it was a university building. It simply had to look differently than a secondary school or a primary school, which could have a much simpler appearance and could be dimensioned much more modestly.

The character of the building is a question of societal positioning, of the function of the building and also the intention of the client.'

One thing I know about the psychology of architects is that they work from what they know. In the nineteenth century, architects were given completely new kinds of commissions, which led to strained situations because no references were available. What did architects do about designing the character of these new buildings?

'These new commissions demanded a great deal of creativity. Things did not always go well. The eclectic architect Jan Leliman once made a design for the Rijksmuseum. At that time it was still called Museum Willem I. It was a design like no other. It was conceived out of the blue, and you can immediately see that it doesn't work.

Regarding the character of the building, an architect must elaborate on what is already there. Even if he goes against what is currently there: if it always used to be black, now he wants to make it white. Brilliant. But in any case there must be a point of reference.'

So the character of the building depends on the function of the building. The richness of ornament illustrates the social status of that function. In which way was the actual function of the building made

Museum Willem I in Amsterdam by Jan Leliman (1865)

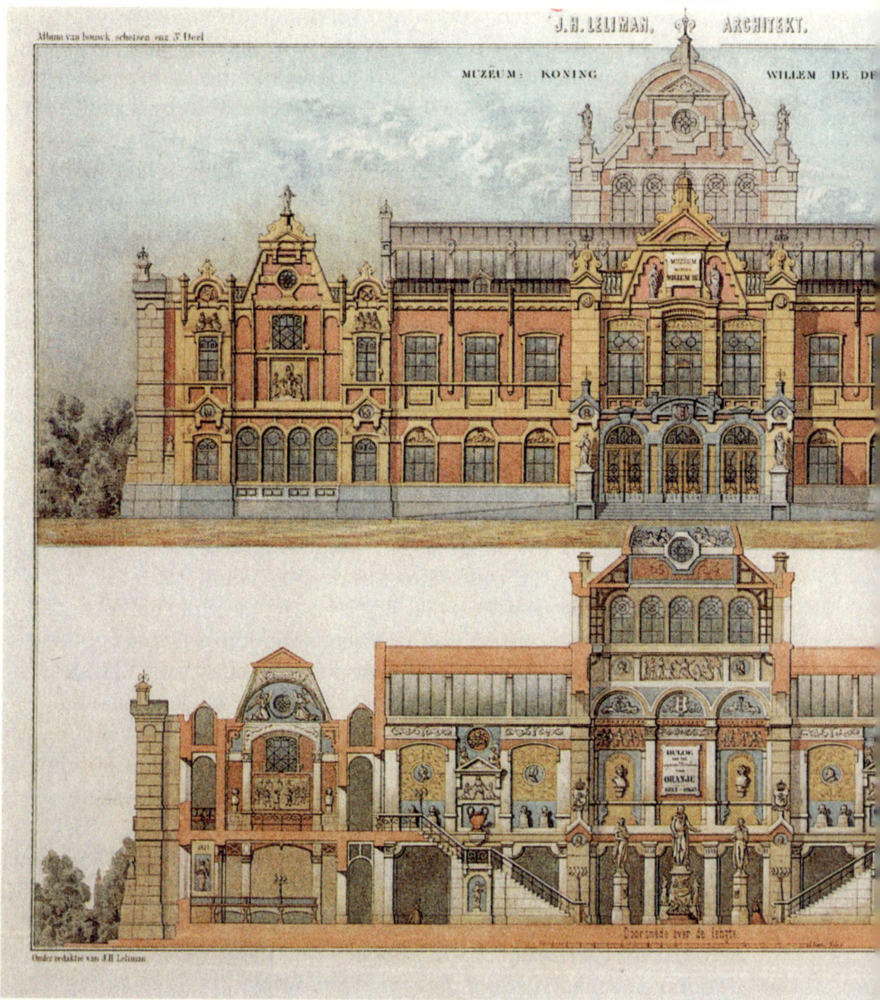

clear? Did the text on the façade also play a role in this regard? A text which, for example in the work of Robert Venturi and Denise Scott Brown, at a certain point became enormously enlarged?

'The text sometimes plays a role, certainly. Here we are talking about character, but also about truth. Sometimes they are very close to one another. Here we come into the area of truth. That which is expressed in the façade must be in accordance with what a building is. One cannot lie about this. The expression of the function of a building can take place with relatively simple means, which is the case with the text.

An orphanage, for example, cannot be recognized directly as such. Based on the character of the building itself, you could just as easily think that it was a hospital or a residential community. However, the gate of an orphanage always portrays the figures of a raggedly clothed little boy and little girl. Consequently, you can always see that it is an orphanage.

If you go yet another step, you come to a subtle aspect that even today is only understood by architects. For example, how can you distinguish a hospital from a seminary? These are both large buildings with many tall windows. The public would be unable to see the difference between these buildings. But architects, who look more discerningly, would see an entrance for the ambulance at the hospital, which a seminary does not have. In that case, you are no longer referring to the character at the level of the ornament, but to the level of the composition of the building.'

As a rule, ornament represents a virtue. Do you know any examples from the nineteenth century in which ornament represents a vice?

'Do you mean, for example, that ornament was not intended to elevate, but to punish? Of course there are examples of the latter. In the Netherlands, most prisons were designed by father and son Metselaar. All these prisons have the character of a punishment facility. Literally. They all look like fortresses.

The study of character originated in eighteenth century France. This is actually about psychology: what do you feel when you see a building? And the reverse: how can you, as an architect, direct this experience?

This gradually evolved towards the expression of the function and social position of the building. But it began fairly simply in the eighteenth century, with the characterization of emotions: happy, scared, gloomy, exalted and so on. Things that you can easily name.

A prison should have a somber expression. If you stand in front of a prison, you should have the feeling: I don't want to go in and if I do I would never come out again. This is a character that father and son Metselaar could design extremely well. They designed buildings with very thick walls with shooting slits. Whether this was all necessary for the function of the building, I do not know. The entrance door gave you the impression that once you were locked away, you would never be able to get out again. This illustrates the process of directing the feelings of the observer.'

At the Place de la Bastille in Paris in 1813 a twelve meter high watch-tower in the shape of an elephant was built. Were such designs made more frequently during the nineteenth century?

'Now you're coming to a special category of buildings. When I was working on the book *Waarheid en Karakter*, I encountered an article in an architecture journal in which the authors, who were architects, made scornful remarks about a café that was designed in the form of a beer barrel.

I once studied how American architecture from around the turn of the century was viewed from the Netherlands. You see a similar response in that case. From the European perspective, the Americans were just fooling around. The architects on the other side of the Atlantic were not restricted by any theoretical notions whatsoever. The reception of this architecture in the Netherlands was therefore always negative.

A good architect does not work in the midst of his or her professional field, but on the edge. However, an architect cannot venture over this edge; he or she must not leave the field. If you design a building in the form of an elephant, then you do leave the field. You can design something like that only with irony. It must always remain a building. First and foremost.'

Otherwise you could be expelled from the professional community?

'Yes. If you look at the Guggenheim Museum by architect Frank Gehry, for example, it is a building you could associate with everything, a colossal caterpillar, for example. But it should never become that association.'

So it should not be too literal?

'Exactly. And if becomes too literal, then it becomes childish. You must play the game, it must remain intelligent. As an architect, you can evoke an association with the public, but you cannot go too far.

As with other professional communities, in the community of architects there are very subtle rules with which the group distinguishes itself from other groups. These rules are so subtle that they are almost impossible to put into writing. However, everyone understands them.'

How do you see the return of ornament in contemporary architecture?

'If you are referring, for example, to a building in the shape of a W, then you cannot disregard Robert Venturi and Denise Scott Brown. Their contribution is unbelievably important. In their book *Learning from Las Vegas*, they do not refer to a building in the shape of a W, but to a building in the shape of a duck. But that is, of course, what it is. It is impossible to look at it differently than how they have written about it.

With respect to the nineteenth century, I have also learned a great deal from Venturi and Scott Brown. It was only when I read their book that I understood the long line between the current era, Postmodernism and the nineteenth century. In the 1980s, the modernists and the anti-modernists were directly opposed to one another in the Netherlands. Only afterwards a tremendous creativity was unleashed. Charles Jencks is one of those who played an important role in this, by demonstrating this new freedom to the world.'

What are your thoughts about a building in the shape of a W?

It's about the same as a building in the shape of a duck. What else can I say?' (laughs)

You could disapprove of it.

'Yes, you could.' (laughs)

You laugh about it?

'Yes, I have to laugh. Everybody is free to do what they want, of course. Free to choose. I'm not very concerned about that. But if you ask me: what does it take to design a beautiful and important building? Then I think you need more than designing a building in the shape of a giant W.

But perhaps I'm not taking this design as seriously as I should. Perhaps it has a very clever organization. That is certainly possible. But architecture will always be about something more than making a functional building. This has to do with the edge of the professional field, but also with that strange phenomenon of quality. Some things matter, and some things do not. It remains complicated.'

Interview Denise Scott Brown

'We found out that communication was an important factor in the auto city and a basic function of architecture'

Conseil General building in Toulouse, France, by Venturi Scott Brown and Associates (1999)

Denise Scott Brown (1931) is an American architect and principal of Venturi Scott Brown Associates (VSBA) in Philadelphia. Together with her partner in both work and life, Robert Venturi, they have built projects all over the world and have written extensively together.

In 1966, Venturi published a monograph, *Complexity and Contradiction in Architecture*, followed in 1972 by *Learning from Las Vegas*, with Scott Brown and Steven Izenour. In 2004 Scott Brown and Venturi published *Architecture as Signs and Systems for a Mannerist Time*. In 2009 Scott Brown published an essay bundle *Having Words*. Decoration is a prominent aspect in both their architecture and writing.

I speak with Scott Brown in London in 2011, where she is lecturing at the Victoria & Albert Museum as part of a show on Postmodernism, which features the work of VSBA. 'Bob apologizes,' she says, 'at his age he is reluctant to travel, but I still enjoy it.'

I start off the interview by showing her some recent examples of iconographic architecture, such as the Walter Tower, designed by BIG.

What do you think of this contemporary architecture?

'What types of proclamations should private buildings make? For example, why do the homes in this apartment building form a big W? W for what? A home should be part cave, yet where is the sense of shelter here? Why not transmit public messages via public or civic buildings, or through modest ornament on private front doors and community entrances?'

Should ornament be used only in public buildings?

'No, but it might apply differently to them. Traditionally, civic buildings have looked differently than houses and commercial buildings. They had unusual silhouettes, often with domes, and larger building components, wider structural spans, and more expensive and durable materials. These differences caused scale relationships in civic architecture to be larger and more violent – the jump, for example, between the monumental cathedral door and the small door cut into it for everyday use. Decoration on such buildings conveyed public and civic meanings, and could evoke the private meanings of individuals and subgroups.'

In the nineteenth century, a building's composition, more than its ornament, suggested its functions. In this respect, do you feel that silhouette was key?

'Perhaps, and if composition could explain function, ornament could comment on structure, especially in the classical orders. But mostly it conveyed religious or cultural messages and civic and national pride. Modernists thought they had done away with all that, but they, in fact, applied symbolism to all buildings – industrial symbolism. And because *Learning from Las Vegas* documents the inescapability of reference despite these attempts, we subtitled it *The Forgotten Symbolism of Architectural Form*.'

Where does this lead you as a self-proclaimed Modernist?

'Bob and I try to design appropriate architecture; "proper", "*comme il faut*" edifices that are frequently (but not always) "ugly and ordinary". To do this we consider archetypes. Most buildings – houses, housing, offices, labs, fire stations, churches, theaters – fit within generic types, for example the row house, the palazzo, the basilica, the loft, the market. And for each type there is an example *par excellence,* an essence – an archetype. In 1960s Las Vegas, The Strip was the archetype of all strips.'

How do you find the archetype?

'You may search anywhere, but mythology may most clearly convey it. Toys and storybooks are a source. For some United States archetypes, imagine a toy train town. What would its store, post office, town hall, school and houses be like? The elementary school, for example, would be a four-square building, flat-roofed with corner windows and a flag at the entrance. Although there are other models, most Americans know this one. In designing a school you need not imitate the archetype, but you should keep it in mind, along with your other loves and images – of Aalto? Michelangelo? – as you work to satisfy the brief.

Inntel Hotel in Zaandstad, the Netherlands, by WAM architects (2006-2010)

Our Learning from Levittown studio was research-oriented, but it included a short sketch design phase where one topic was: "Do for housing what Oldenburg did for hamburgers." One team envisioned a giant Levittown house. The garage door held an apartment, the front windows two more, and so on. For the final jury, students made a soft model of their house; a cake, which we all ate afterwards. It was a joke, but who knows where such ideas can lead?'

Near Amsterdam there is a hotel by WAM Architects that looks like a stack of traditional Dutch houses. And the VitraHaus in Weil amRhein by Herzog & De Meuron is an abstracted version of the same idea.

Can you give an example of how you play with an archetype?

'In the mid-1960s Bob designed Fire Station 4 in Columbus, Ohio. Generically, it was a garage for fire engines, a drying tower for hoses, and a home-away-from-home for firefighters. Expressively, it was a small, red brick civic building with a big and solemn function. Archetypally, it was a civic palazzo with a tower, but a modest one, whose suburban site contravened the archetype, and whose functional requirements produced a façade that was too wide by Renaissance standards for the height of its tower. Bob therefore added a white brick appliqué to the offending façade to suggest the outline of a traditional palazzo. And, given its residential activities and location and Bob's love of scale jumps, he posed the domestic windows of the living quarters against the big engine door. And instead of a bell or clock he put a big 4 at the top of the tower. This decoration gave important public information, referred to history, tipped our hat to Pop Art, and illustrates our approach to decoration in civic architecture.'

Does ornament, or decoration as you call it, always idealize what the building is about?

'For us, decoration is one type of ornament. Both involve symbols and communication, but they don't necessarily idealize a building's function or meaning. And the archetype represents an essence, the most cogent example, rather than an ideal.'

Although their designs relate to the archetype, Venturi and Scott Brown avoid approaching it too closely. They appear more comfortable maintaining a distance, making ironic comments about the archetype and dramatizing conflicts between the archetype and the specific requirements of the commission. The same goes for the tension that arises between the decoration that suits the archetype and modern construction. The architects seem to feel that, by working with the disparity, they can be more honest than they would in designing "harmonious" architecture where tensions are "falsely" suppressed.

It seems to me that you like to show, even exaggerate, tensions that arise in compositions.

'In life, archetypes must usually be compromised by impinging forces from other realities, therefore they are impure. But you're right: we prefer them that way. August Perret believed that ornament always hid a flaw in construction. It shielded spots where shrinkage might occur or weather might penetrate. Accepting the flaws might sound terrible, but in life not all imperfections can be avoided. So, Modernist pejoratives notwithstanding, the "dishonesty" of decoration is not necessarily a sin. Perret's ornament prevented the fault from affecting the rest of the building. Bob's ornament showed the shape he would have liked within the one he had to have. In both cases ornament resulted from the interplay of "is" and "ought" – between what we would like and what we must accept. In choosing this interplay we are

Fire Station 4 in Columbus, USA, by Venturi Scott Brown and Associates (1968)

Vanna Venturi House in Chestnut Hill, USA, by Venturi Scott Brown and Associates (1964)

acting within the social and moral mandates of Postmodernism as they evolved during and after World War II. Yet the ironic modulating of the red brick with the white derives as well from Mannerism. It's a mannerist grin, but a loving one, respectful of what being human means. Mannerism helps to accommodate conflict – often between urban systems – and it prevents the civic from being too monumental.'

How is the ornament – decoration – established in your work?

'Decoration was historically related to the technology of its time. For example, Ancient Egyptian clay writing tablets became stone hieroglyphs. It was used largely for communication, about gods, kings, states and people. And it had multifaceted relationships with its containing architecture. Early Christian wall frescoes were flat, but with the rediscovery of Antiquity, relief reappeared. Renaissance decoration required about 30 cm of depth and Baroque perhaps a meter. Rococo frizzled up, its relief was often less than a centimeter deep. Modern architecture, too, in mandating abstraction cleaved to flatness. Modernist fiat abolished decoration. But it crept back in their handcrafted "machine" forms and surfaces designed to look machined. And formalism re-entered when they defined Cubist forms as the functional vocabulary of the future.

Postmodernism as it evolved in the 1950s and 1960s, and until its 1980s cooption by PoMo, had diverse strands – social, moral and aesthetic – and our view of ornament in architecture derived from several of them. The fight for social justice during the Civil Rights movement taught us to respect values and tastes other than our own and to re-estimate our views on urbanism. Opening ourselves to popular culture, conventional building and the landscape of strip and sprawl, including even the neon of Las Vegas, we found out that communication was an important factor in the auto city and a basic function of architecture. All these, and seeing architectural history in a new light, reinforced our interest in ornament. We analyzed its role in traditional architecture and tried to apply what we learned. Updating Modernism to suit today's needs, including its dire social needs, sent us on a search for "ugly and ordinary" rather than "heroic and original" architecture and reinforced our interest in observing the technics of everyday architecture.

While researching ornament we learned from redecorating our own home. Starting as Art Nouveau of 1909, it became, like most architects' houses, a lab for experiments to be toned down in later work for clients. But we did not remove its interiors in the Modern way. We chose and designed furniture and objects, but mostly we applied pattern, and continued our research into the ordinary in fabric and wallpaper showrooms. Another source of learning was from the developers' calculus of decoration. For them, almost everything is rentable – up to but not including the first centimeter in from the building perimeter. This thin layer is available for decoration, but nothing can be done that will remove floor space or affect optimum window spacing for offices. The cladding has become packaging.

This outlook was reflected in our design for the Best Showroom, which we covered in a large-scale floral wrap. Its pattern, a symbolic if ironic civic communication, derived from bedroom wallpaper in our house, but we radically altered its scale and repeat. The Best Pattern led in turn to the Grandmother Flowers of our Knoll chairs and fabrics.

I continued my research into the ordinary via façade gazing, considering building walls in relation to local traditions, technologies of the time, functional needs, and the requirements of context. Long urban streets are my laboratories and those of Geneva offer a good testing ground. Outside the city center, arterials walled by residential and commercial buildings six or seven stories high stretch into the hinterland. Each reveals its era-based, moderate-cost construction techniques, and because Geneva was never bombed, you can see the evolution of the "Orders" of its everyday architecture over time and space.

When Beaux-Arts architecture students drafted and rendered the Greek and Roman Orders, they were examining wall systems; architects today do the same when they consider how functional requirements and the need for shelter will call for a particular structural system, then how this will be designed and detailed to admit people, things, air and light, mediate temperature, emit information, and be sustainable. Searching for the Orders for today and doing so specifically for each of our projects is one of the reasons for my façade gazing.

Consider Dutch and English seventeenth and eighteenth-century architecture. Given the difficulties of pre-industrial land travel, the two countries established closer relations with each other across the sea than they had with their

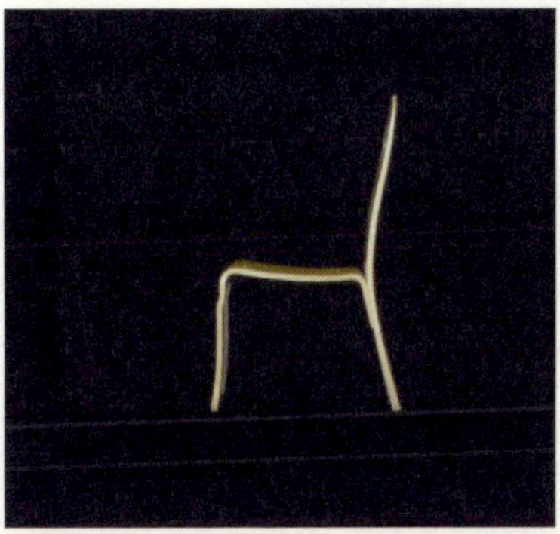

Knoll furniture design by Venturi Scott Brown and Associates (1984)

Auditorium of the Conseil General building

Two office towers in Shanghai by Venturi Scott Brown and Associates (2003)

Interior of the auditorium of the Conseil General building

Entrance of the Conseil General building in Toulouse, France, by Venturi Scott Brown and Associates (1999)

hinterlands. Therefore English and Dutch building of the era had much in common. Each evolved a brick architecture from local clay, and derived from it a rich Georgian townhouse tradition. But in Dutch pile-driven construction, spans were narrower and windows more closely spaced than the English. Moving to the Eastern part of the United States, Philadelphia colonial architecture picks up English proportions and New York the Dutch. Windows read as punched-in holes in Philadelphia's relatively generous brick walls. In New York the walls between windows are narrower and facades tend to be framed and paneled.'

New York was of course founded by the Dutch as New Amsterdam.

'That's right.

In 2007, when designing Lenfest Hall, a new building for the Curtis Institute in Philadelphia, we had to find an architecture that would feel civic and serve the modern needs of this great school of music, and yet fit in with the spirit of Philadelphia and complement the historic mix of styles and eras on Locust Street. This seemed unimaginable till we remembered the Conservatory of Music in Amsterdam, a brick building whose tall, narrow windows were monumental and civic, and yet did not jar the scale of the neighborhood.'

How do the contemporary orders of architecture translate into your own work?

'In our projects, we look for contemporary ways of responding to the local orders. We try to go with conventional building methods of the region but may push them a little, asking how far can "ought" diverge from "is"? That's the challenge and the fun. Yet we know too, that a Modern vernacular – loosely based on the International Style – has spread across the globe: the Moderns were right, but would they be happy?

In America we have built mostly for academic and civic institutions, where steel structures with masonry and drywall cladding and infilling are usually indicated. But in our Conseil General building in Toulouse, the French equivalent of a State capitol, the structural framework and infill are in concrete of different types and cladding is of local red brick and limestone.'

How does the decoration in your work fit into this?

'I had been studying signs as urban communication before I came to America. Our *Learning from Las Vegas* research was a continuation of that interest. Then, when we started to use our research in design, the developers' model and 1960s neon produced our best exemplars. In search of decoration without depth, I revisited Art Deco bas-relief. Like the Rococo, it might take up one centimeter, but in that dimension Deco could depict six receding surfaces. Nevertheless, even one centimeter was too deep, and we decided that our ornament, being modern, should have zero depth – also that it should not reproduce traditional forms, although it could sometimes represent them via allusion or suggest depth via illusion. So we turned to flat sources, to wallpapers, Victorian pattern books and the Deco poster art of E. McKnight Kauffer. This resulted in our Best, Knoll, ISI, Brand, Grandmother and Notebook patterns, as well as those in our house and many that were not built. But neon was more riveting and we started designing facades that emit light.

In 1995 Bob designed two point blocks in China. He applied red neon decoration to their Miesian fronts and together they depict a Chinese pagoda. Very mannerist. We had watched the destruction of 1960s Las Vegas neon with sorrow and noted that the free forms hoped for from LED, to help it achieve a baroque ebullience, did not materialize. Despite their vastness, the rectangularity of LED signs and their paleness when seen from a distance, reduce rather than augment their supporting buildings.'

In your work you often put exuberant decoration on relatively modest buildings. Is that not a paradox? Should modest architecture not have modest decoration?

'Not when the decoration aids the functioning of the building or the street. We were dismayed by the speciousness of PoMo commercial architecture but were intrigued by the commercialism of 1960 Las Vegas. It was talented. Even if we had moral questions about gambling and grossly expensive buildings, they had flair. And their electrographics supported their purpose.

Dave Crane, my studio teacher and advisor at Penn University, talked about the Four Faces of Movement. For him, the street was not only a route for traffic, it was a room for activities, it provided access to buildings and land. Therefore it helped to build the city, and it was a conveyer of communication. He suggested three ways in which it performed its communication functions, and one was through signs. Even on a modest building such signs may be exuberant if they are in an exuberant location or serve an exuberant purpose.'

Your design for the Philadelphia Orchestra Hall is fascinating. The music notes on the façade eloquently explain the purpose of the building.

'They came from the Moonlight Sonata. But we rationalized the notes to make them simpler to read and construct, and we projected them across the whole façade.'

Are your big signs always welcomed by your clients?

'No. Though in some projects big signs are part of the brief, the clients want them. But successor clients for Orchestra Hall did not, and trouble can occur with signs on campuses.

For a Princeton project we argued that lettering of modest size – but too widely spaced for the regulations – was appropriate for its purpose and location. We pointed out to borough authorities that the project was at the center of the campus, away from the public and that

Frist Campus Center at the campus of Princeton University, USA, by Venturi Scott Brown and Associates (2000)

driving at 35 miles an hour on the tree-lined edge road, you might just see it for two seconds. But we still had to remove it. Yet protuberances remained where individual letters were to rise above the entrance. Now students can be seen explaining to guests that the strange shapes in the stone profile are the tops of letters that spell Frist Campus Center.

At the Episcopal Academy outside Philadelphia, a large sign was needed, to read from across the parking lot at a major entrance to the school. A side wall of the chapel we were designing there was a perfect spot for it. We theorized that a big sign with fat letters for visibility could

Philadelphia Orchestra Hall, USA, by Venturi Scott Brown and Associates (1996)

be acceptable if it was incised in the masonry in low relief. And it was.

At The Curtis Institute for Music the sign runs the length of our Dutch-Georgian façade and reads as if it were an entablature. Again in low relief, and incised in red stone, it tones with the red brick, and no one has objected.'

Let's go back in time again. I am curious how your architecture was received in the seventies.

'For a while we were part of high culture, whether we agreed to be or not, and we worked simultaneously for firefighters, a low-income community combatting an expressway, museum directors and art collectors.'

Wasn't there criticism at that time on the incorporation of popular culture into architecture? Didn't people find your approach too literal to be considered architecture?

'There was enormous criticism. For two generations, architects saw our role as putting a moustache on the Mona Lisa. When I told architects of my generation and the next that *Learning from Las Vegas* was in part a social tract, they would say, "You've got to be kidding!" But today's young architects reply: "We know that!" The present generation is energetically reappraising our work, fleshing out all its dimensions. We finally feel known as we really are.'

In *Learning from Las Vegas*, Scott Brown and Venturi identified two approaches to signing in architecture, the Duck and the Decorated Shed. The Duck derived from a roadside store near New York that sold a regional specialty, Long Island duckling, and was shaped like a duck. But most commercial strip buildings, like those in and around Las Vegas, were simple boxes with signs on them or at their road frontages, i.e. Decorated Sheds. Here, a store selling duck would display a large, flat sign with words and duck graphics.

Following this principle, buildings with an iconography that has shaped their exterior can be called Ducks; buildings with an iconography that has shaped flat signs on it or next to it can be called Decorated Sheds. The Duck and the Decorated Shed define the outer ends of a wide spectrum. Within it some buildings can be more Duck and others more Decorated Shed.

According to Venturi and Scott Brown, the Decorated Shed has a functional interior and a repetitive, cost efficient construction. The Duck is the opposite; its complex exterior form negatively affects the functionality of its interior, making its construction more expensive. For most buildings, Venturi and Scott Brown therefore prefer the Decorated Shed.

Most of your projects could indeed be called Decorated Sheds. Have you ever designed a Duck?

'Designers of the Long Island duck obviously felt that informing

The Curtis Institute for Music, Lenfest Hall, in Philadelphia, USA, by Venturi Scott Brown and Associates (2011)

Interior of the Lenfest Hall

Episcopal Academy Chapel in Newtown Square, USA, by Venturi Scott Brown and Associates (2008)

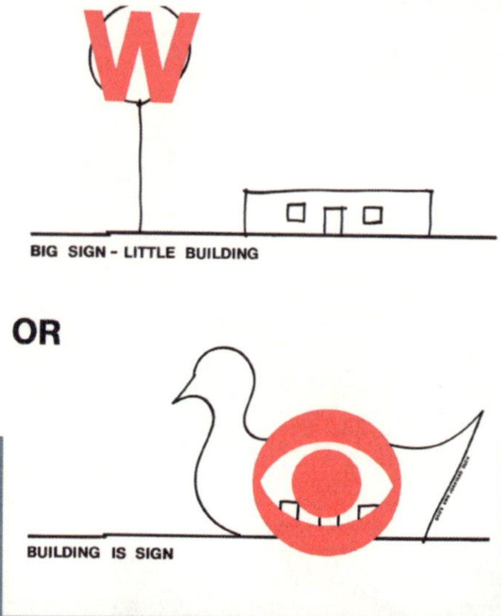

Decorated Shed versus Duck

The duck restaurant on Long Island, New York, as discovered in the early seventies

passersby of the delectable food on sale there was more important than making the kitchen work perfectly. So if your question means "Have you ever designed a building where the outside functions were more important than the inside?" The answer is "Yes, but . . ."

We are not always against Ducks. Historically some buildings, particularly civic and institutional ones, the Parthenon, for example, had to be Ducks, and this holds for today. However ours in that category turn out part Duck and part Decorated Shed.'

Could you explain one of your designs for a Duck?

'Our Episcopal Academy Chapel is literally and figuratively central

to the life of its K-12 school, and its form symbolizes its faith. Therefore it's a Duck – although its duck qualities tend to fall apart as you enter it.

All divisions of the school face onto a green and we were asked to place the chapel centrally at its head. Although Christian worship stresses personal communion with God, people wanted to see each other as well as the altar. So the chapel plan is semi-circular. Nevertheless we kept the focus toward the altar and the aspiration upward toward the light and the spire. And several layers of clerestory lighting encircle the perimeter, providing the transcendence called for in church roofs. The main entrance on the green is through an arcade whose silhouette and ornament comment succinctly on church architecture, even though it is only a flat screen. From a distance the spire suggests a country church nestled in the landscape, from the curves of the entry road it is a beacon to the heart of the school. But it is merely two intersecting cross-walls, braced by each other and tapering as they rise to outline a steeple. Near the top the crevice they form is reamed to make space for the bell, but the sound comes from elsewhere.

The building's church shape is formed by flat sheets. They define the spire and hall, and mount to suggest a sloping sanctuary lit by clerestories. They make light that seems magic yet provide a realistic building that the school can afford: one of masonry, striped "streaky-bacon"-style in light and dark gray.

Yet this is one of the most abstract buildings we have designed. The school resisted iconography beyond the arcade and a cross above the altar; and we agreed because the chapel was to nurture the spirituality of all the community, and children of all faiths were to feel welcome in it. There's much more to say about the chapel design but I'm focusing here on ornament.'

I see the ornament as an explanation of the buildings' function, structure, organization, status, et cetera. Do you recognize that notion?

'That is one of its functions. But architecture has traditionally also communicated the power of its client, often the king or the church, sometimes the sovereign people. Social scientists and politicians would ask "communicate with whom?" and they would reject the naïve Modernists' reply "with the masses". But if groups can now be disaggregated via cable TV and social media, why can't decoration be tuned to subgroup meanings? Or can it evoke both shared meaning and the personal associations of individuals?

Architects tend to communicate with each other via their buildings, and this is called elitist. But granted that we must dialogue with the public or publics, is conducting a parallel in-group conversation wrong if it doesn't impede the functioning of the building or cost too much?

We recently designed a building that everyone fought: neighbors, preservationists, and the public. When they found our brick sidewall too plain, I whispered to Bob that we should do as they asked and provide a pattern – one that does this (puts up her middle finger).'

That ornament could explain the troubled birth of the building.

'I don't think the project will go ahead, but for reasons to do with the economy.'

MVRDV designed a housing block in Lyon that displays the first sentences of the European Constitution. When the French voted against the constitution in a referendum, architect Winy Maas became very angry and decided to include this text on the building as a protest.

'There have always been engravings incised on buildings. And they always became outdated. But they witness the history of the building. And people will understand Maas's protest ten years from now. After that it may still mean something and look good. LED can get a message onto a building in minutes and remove it again as quickly. Graffiti, once *the* inscriptions of protest, now establish turf. It's fascinating that graffiti artists adjust their inscriptions to the perception distances of their viewers and to the informal panels and entablatures they inherit – bridge abutments and expressway ramp edges – much as traditional stone engravers do.'

You mentioned an ornament in the form of an abstracted middle finger. Are there limitations to what you can do?

'This was a joke bred of exasperation. I spent years in community participation with low-income inner-city people trying to save their neighborhoods from an expressway. They taught me so much and I was left with unending admiration for their acumen in handling their tricky situation. But here we were dealing with the educated lay public, professionals who came with their lawyers intending to protect their property values. In my experience, upper middle class participation includes people with passion for their community, but it also abounds in demagoguery, private agendas posing as public interest, and ancient art class experience offered as proof of design knowledge.

I doubt I would incise a finger in a wall pattern, but if I did, it would be unrecognizable. A mannerist tic, a private joke, its humor would dull the pain without hurting the building. Laughing is better than crying. That's heavy work for a little decoration, but it suggests the emotion that can accompany creating and perceiving in architecture. And it goes without saying that cruel decoration with evil intent – racist symbolism or insignia, for example – is vile and beneath contempt.'

Can architecture be funny?

'Absolutely. Although I would rather it be witty. And you should laugh not *at* but *with* your client. You may, however, laugh a little at yourself.'

Interview
Charles Jencks

'The icon should not remain always enigmatic: architecture has to be more responsible than that'

The Shard in London by Renzo Piano Building Workshop (2000-2012)

Charles Jencks (1939) is a British architecture historian. In his books, Jencks has extensively documented and theorized the emergence and transformation of Postmodernism in architecture. In *The Iconic Building* (2005) Jencks investigated a new kind of building that emerged in the late 1990s and early 2000s. After his wife Maggie died of cancer, Jencks devoted himself to setting up centers for cancer care in her name – Maggie's Cancer Caring Centres – near hospitals throughout Britain. Among the architects who have designed these Maggie's Centres are Rem Koolhaas, Zaha Hadid and Frank Gehry.

The notion of the building as ornament is based on an architectural practice in which a specific iconography is applied in a design to evoke specific associations with the public. In *The Iconic Building,* Jencks puts forward a notion which at first sight might seem comparable to this notion, but in fact differs greatly from it. In his book Jencks calls for the design of enigmatic signifiers: buildings that evoke all sorts of associations with the public. According to Jencks, the enigma results from a society that has lost its certainty about previous signifiers such as religion, progress and political emancipation. With its layered meaning, the enigmatic signifier also has the ability to engage the public for a longer period of time.

When I visit Charles Jencks in his London home he starts off by showing me his brightly colored kitchen: the Indian Summer Room. The room provides cross views through the house. Jencks claims that the eclectic, Postmodernist style of the kitchen is 'more functional than functionalism.' He adds that only 10 per cent of the materials in the room are real, the remainder is simulated. After we sit down, Jencks asks me the first question.

'Your book is about ornament, but you want to talk to me about the icon?'

Yes, the book is about ornament on the scale of the building.

'That is related to the icon. Go ahead.'

When did you first become aware that something like the icon existed?

'For me it started in the sixties when French structuralism, with its semiotics, came to Britain. I was very much involved in that, and we wrote several books on meaning in architecture, etcetera. And from Charles Pierce, the semiotition, I learned that there are three kinds of signs: the icon, the index and the symbol. In brief, the icon is a formal similitude between signifier and signified, the index is a literal imprint of an object, and the symbol is a conventional representation. In all the books I have written on Postmodernism I discuss these three types of signs. The concepts of the duck and the Decorated Sed that Robert Venturi and Denise Scott Brown talk about is a reductive, pop version of two kinds of sign. Both the duck and the high-flyer are iconic signs. My kitchen depicting Indian Summer is obviously a symbolic sign, using conventions from Hindu architecture.

When I wrote *The Iconic Building*, from 2003 to 2005, the icon was at the center stage in the architectural debate. Critics like Deyan Sudjic declared it dead on arrival, but only more icons appeared. My work has been to show that the iconic building has emerged as an ambiguous, enigmatic sign and that it is here to stay. The enigma is necessary in a culture that has lost its direction. There is no common belief, religion or meaning that can be represented. What are architects to do? Architects run away from any explicit and historical iconography, they hide it, and via the enigmatic sign have been able to slip it into the equation.

Erwin Panofsky describes iconography as the conventional sign. If I wear a top hat on St. Patrick's Day, that would be a convention, or iconographic. This conventionalism was accepted by architects. Le Corbusier used the ship and the machine as his iconography. But already before the 1920s, architects had become embarrassed by their conventional signs partly because they changed all the time, with politics and fashion. Instead, they wanted something more permanent, and they mistakenly thought modernism would give it.

Underneath this conventional iconography lies iconology. Iconology is the study of the underlying symbols or symptoms, as Panofsky describes it. To ornament iconology is crucial because it means getting to the deepest level of interpretation, the metanarrative.

I recently finished the book *Fifty years of Postmodernism* and in it I distinguish four degrees of ornament. The first degree is construction and structure. That is the most obvious level. Rem Koolhaas, for instance, ornaments the CCTV Building with structured diagrams in a very amusing way. The second degree is semantics, the meaning of things, what my kitchen is about. The third degree is iconology, ornament as style, and the hidden meaning of things. Something that architects are unconscious about and therefore don't like to talk about. The fourth degree is music, the most important level of ornament.

Façade analysis of the Hotel Fouquet Barrière in Paris by Eduard François (2003-2006)

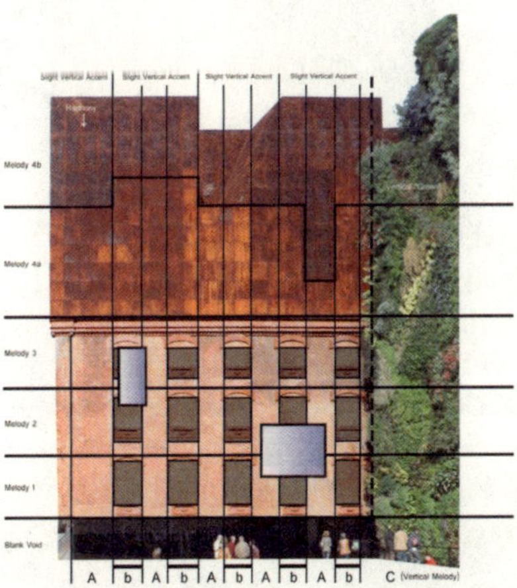

Façade analysis of the Caixa Forum in Madrid by Herzog & de Meuron (2001-2008)

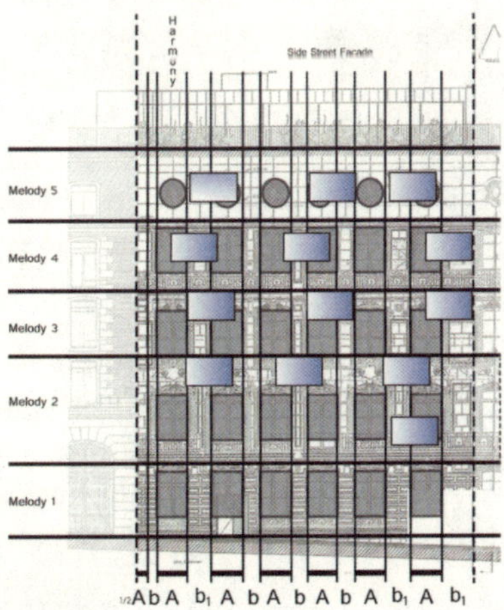

Madrid Barajas Airport by Rogers Stirk Harbour + Partners (1997-2010)

Ravensbourne in London by Foreign Office Architects (2010)

CCTV Building in Beijing by OMA (2002-2012)

In his book *A Sense of Order* E.H. Gombrich ends his discussion of ornament with the musical analogy, a profound point. Architecture is a sensuous medium, very much like frozen music as is said. Architecture, too, has themes, variations, developments, and so on. Music is an intrinsic level of meaning for architects, though no architect has written much about it in forty years.

Each of the four degrees of ornament is important, but collectively they are much more important because together they lead to resonance. However, usually young architects don't have time to think about this, they are trying so hard to get the next job. But an architect like Alejandro Zaero-Polo is almost there, with his design for the Ravensbourne College in London.

I have diagrammed musical ornament in the architecture of Edouard François and Herzog & de Meuron. These are both examples of contextual counterpoint using themes from the existing context and contemplating them in a musical way.'

Following the success of the Guggenheim Museum in Bilbao, many architects were asked by their clients to design a building that would achieve a similar effect. Were the architects that tried to design an icon simply responding to the question at hand, or did they themselves want to design an icon as well?

'That's ambiguous. The right half of their brain, their feminine side, wanted to make icons. But the left half of their brain, the analytical side, resisted that – like society at large. These two sides have been in continuous conflict. It is hard to defend the iconic buildings, because of their failures. The reason that there are so many bad icons is that most architects are not free enough to think about them in a serious and artistic way. So you end up in a double-bind.

I was a judge on the competition for the CCTV Building in Beijing. The client said that it had to result in the Bilbao effect. It had to be an icon. Put a gun to Rem Koolhaas' head and he will do it. The Bird's Nest Stadium that Herzog & de Meuron and Ai Weiwei designed for Beijing also is one of the most extraordinary iconic buildings of our time, like the Coliseum in Rome. Architect Jacques Herzog said, "you want an icon, then I will create one" – very self-consciously. Like Rem Koolhaas, Frank Gehry, Zaha Hadid and others, he knows how to use ambiguity and enigma to create a multi-layered symbol.

But other architects have a hard time designing successful ones, because they are just not artistic or free enough, having been trained in reductive functionalism. The airport that Richard Rogers designed in Madrid, in a way, is a good icon. I am not saying these non-artistic architects can't do it, but they often fail. And they are worried by the demand.'

In your book you interview Norman Foster on his design of the Swiss Re Tower in London, now called the "Gherkin". Do you really think he thought of his building as an icon?

Swiss Re Headquarters in London by Foster + Partners (1997-2004)

Bird's Nest Stadium in Beijing by Herzog & de Meuron with Ai Weiwei (2002-2008)

Palace of Peace and Reconciliation in Astana, Kazakhstan, by Foster + Partners (2004-2006)

'Perhaps he won't publicly admit he designed an egg. But I have a document from his office showing originally it was an egg icon, actually the index of an egg. And then he elongated the form to accommodate more floors, so it became a stretched egg. Maybe he was not fully aware of all the images and meanings he was handling while designing this building, but subconsciously metaphors like the gherkin must have passed through his mind.

I once pointed out to him that the spiraling skycourts could be related to the Fibonacci sequences, like the one you can see in a pineapple. So I gave him one, and he immediately agreed. In his lectures he shows the pinecone on top of St. Paul's Cathedral, which his building is supposed to emulate. No architect had remarked on this pinecone before. In a way, St. Paul's is a pinecone and his Swiss Re Tower is a pinecone.

Foster thinks very quickly about icons, and reduces them, as does Renzo Piano with The Shard.'

But the architects you mention come from such a different tradition that it must be very hard for them to design these buildings.

'They come from an engineering and functionalist tradition that doesn't usually want to admit there is such a thing as iconography. Foster comes from that tradition, but now sees the point of iconography, and has designed a pyramid for Kazakhstan. The pyramid form was an idea of the president of Kazakhstan. But Foster clearly knows how to handle such an iconic form.'

Does iconic architecture require a new kind of architect?

'Yes. But we also need new theories of communication. We can now teach architects how to design good icons as enigmatic and multifunctional objects. Clients will keep asking for them, so we better get better at designing them. Fast.'

Do enigmatic signifiers, as you call them, not always end up having one dominant meaning? Like the Gherkin or the Bird's Nest Stadium? And would it therefore not be smarter if architects simply designed this dominant metaphor? Like the building in the shape of a W that BIG recently designed?

'A dominant metaphor along with a lot of subtle metaphors is a possible strategy. The Bird's Nest Stadium designed by Herzog & de Meuron and Ai Weiwei relates to a lot of other things too, which is why it's so interesting. A W, however, tends to be just a W.

In the 1970s there was a very famous women's wear magazine called W. The people who know that might think of the "W" as a metaphor for women or women's wear. So it might be misunderstood.'

What fascinates me about architectural firms like Neutelings Riedijk and MVRDV is that they try to steer the perception of the public by choosing a single iconography and aim to make this iconography somewhat more explicit – more literal – than we are used to.

'Religion used to help people decide what to do, especially those clients who wanted to spend a half a billion dollars. But with the decline of major narratives, architects are at a loss of what to signify. As the art critic Arthur Danto famously said about art, "today it can be anything". It can be anything.

That is one reason why we have to find an iconography that is based on a new common ground. What we all have in common is nature and the cosmos, and these have become a kind of hidden code – the iconology, as I have said in numerous books. But besides being an implicit code, nature and the cosmos should be explicit too.

In effect, the icon should not remain always enigmatic. Architecture has to be more responsible than that, more explicit – and that means dealing with iconography and iconology. Yet nobody can singlehandedly change the ruling fashion, all you can do is to propose an alternative.

What you rightfully point out is that architecture is a public art and that architects are responsible for the iconography and the way these projects communicate. Architects have to be more responsible, but like the pluralist, agnostic society, they are confused on the issues. This confusion leads to the enigmatic signifier and can be evasive.'

DNA Double Helix Sculpture in Cambridge, UK, designed by Charles Jencks (2005)

You often talk about the cosmos as a new source for iconography. But there are plenty of examples in which totally different iconographies have been applied. Neutelings Riedijk, for instance, designed a building that relates to harbor cranes and shipping containers.

'No question, most iconic buildings don't have a natural or cosmic iconography. But a lot of them do, as a hidden code. And it comes back more to iconology than iconography. Peter Eisenman chides me for talking about cosmology, and I understand his misgivings. We want life to be more than nature, more than the cosmos. We want cross coding. It would be boring if everything were cosmic. But if we are spending the public's money, then let's make something that lasts. Nature and the cosmos form the best basis for this.

Various landscapes and sculptures I have designed look at what the permanent icons of the universe are. Such as DNA – the double helix. The whole process of the universe is an icon. The black hole and galaxy are icons, and cosmogenesis will be around forever, right? So if you are an architect and work on iconography, and iconology, why not pick up the universe? You don't have to imitate these icons, you can simply adopt some of their languages, and mix these with other local languages, like harbor cranes. Because the depth comes from the mixing.'

At a certain point in your book you also say that when an iconography becomes too literal, it becomes reductive.

'Everybody feels that.'

But what exactly is too literal? Adriaan Geuze calls it Disney.

'Disney gets boring because the signs are one-liners, without ambiguity, like denotative stop signs.'

So you need a certain abstraction in the iconography?

'Yes, but even more, you need multiple meaning, symbolic architecture with connotations. As a designer you have to slip your piece of architecture into that space of multiple meaning and then, if you're lucky, on the right day, you can create a symbol that resonates with the other areas of building: ornament and light. The Gherkin is a successful example of an icon, with multiple enigmatic metaphors, integrated with the structure, construction and the semantics of an office building.'

Do you think architects should discuss the possible metaphors for a building in their offices? And possibly even test the buildings on an audience?

'Architects should be explicit about that, and discuss the metaphors with each other and with the public. It is a search, and you can only do that with conviction when you include the public and other architects in the process. The constant drawing of metaphors, of iconographies, is not enough, and is only the departure point. It also has to be creative, new, visually exciting, and has to perform a function.'

There are some architects, like Zaha Hadid, who design freeform buildings and describe them as landscapes, clouds and so on. Do you consider this architecture to be iconic as well?

'Yes, and I witnessed an amusing moment – at a meeting on the new book by her partner Patrick Schumacher – when it became explicit. Shortly after Zaha entered the room, Jeff Kipnis wickedly noted that today architects drop pebbles into Chinese riversides and call them buildings. Everybody roared with laughter, and Hadid thought it was funny too.

But when you recall this, you realize that something interesting had happened. In both the popular and professional press it was said that she thought of these Chinese buildings as pebbles, as rocks. Hadid meant it as a metaphor and designed it as a public one. She has come a long way. I haven't visited the buildings yet so I can't say whether they are good iconic buildings or not. Ten years ago Hadid would have kept her head below the parapet and wouldn't have said anything about the metaphor she meant – or used – in her design, and instead talked

Guangzhou Opera House, China, by Zaha Hadid Architects (2003-2010)

Extension to the Denver Art Museum, USA, by Studio Daniel Libeskind (2006)

Royal Ontario Museum in Toronto by Studio Daniel Libeskind (2007)

about urban landscapes. But now we can discuss this with her: why did you want to make a rock, is the end result rock enough, and how does the public perceive it?

There is one metaphor I find difficult to understand. Zaha Hadid and Daniel Libeskind have designed a couple of "crystal" buildings. The Maggie's Centre that she has designed for us is an example. Real crystals go from big to small, in a kind of transformation, but the crystal metaphors that Hadid, and Libeskind likewise, design remain crude in their faceting. They miss a fractal dimension; they don't scale down. Why not? Is it more expensive? Or do architects not have the conviction or energy to carry out the design idea at bigger and smaller scales? Or aren't they being asked to design their crystals all the way? With designs like the Ontario Museum in Toronto or City Centre in Las Vegas, you realize that Daniel Libeskind is exploiting the iconic side of the crystal, but is not carrying the metaphor through in details, which would give it greater resonance.'

There has always been lots of criticism of the icon. Some critics have used the recession that occurred in America and Europe after 2007 as an opportunity to declare the icon dead. Do you understand this discontent about the icon?

'Ninety-five percent of iconic buildings are failures, because we lack an iconography and an iconology, and the artistic conviction to carry metaphors through. It's not just the financial crisis, Disneyland or the urban problems that create the cityscape of a World's Fair.'

As I understand it, some of the criticism is also that icons are too impractical and too capitalist.

'But remember the many iconic monsters were produced under communism from 1960-1990, from Russia to China to East Asia. The City of Culture that Peter Eisenman designed for Santiago de la Compostela

Crystals at City Center in Las Vegas by Studio Daniel Libeskind (2009)

recently got flamed in the press. There are now even people that blame Eisenman, and Santiago Calatrava too, for the debt that Spain is in. They forget that architects are very minor players in the meltdown, though the property market is one of the big causes of the crunch.

In late capitalism, the average iconic buildings can cost half a billion dollars, or at least twice the cost in real terms of the 1960s iconic buildings. And each city wants one. Architects take enormous risks with this money.

But this is the inflationary reality. We live in a celebrity culture, under late capitalism, and the commissions are too big. You can try, like Peter Eisenman, to put this building underground, but half a billion dollars is not going to disappear. Nor will the iconic building. It's only getting stronger. For the critics there is only one conclusion: we must learn how to design better icons and fight for them. With the client, with society, with the media. It won't be easy, but who said architecture was easy?

The other night Rem Koolhaas told me about a Hong Kong competition he had lost to Norman Foster. The competition is fierce. At the same time they are competing in the Middle East over very interesting, dense, ecological cities. Norman Foster has designed Masdar City in Abu Dhabi; Rem Koolhaas designed the City in the Desert for another one of the United Arab Emirates. That's good, positive. So late capitalism isn't all bad.'

And the icon with its iconography is definitely not the only theme in contemporary architecture.

'Exactly. There are probably six or so other competing traditions as well.'

How do you regard the future of the icon? Will most new icons be built in the Middle East and Asia?

'No, they will be built everywhere. In London, during the biggest economic crisis in years, four iconic buildings are being built: the walkie-talkie, the cheese grater, the pinnacle and The Shard.

So the icon is not going away?

'Not a chance.'

City of Culture of Galicia in Santiago de la Compostela, Spain, by Eisenman Architects (from 1999 onwards)

Masdar City in Abu Dhabi, UAE, by Foster + Partners (2007-2008)

City in the Desert in the United Arab Emirates by OMA (2006)

Collage Alphabet

The BE buildings in Brussels by JDS (2007)

'HvH' for the Dutch municipality Hoek van Holland, 'VEJLE for the Danish city Vejle, 'Y' as an ironic reference to the Amsterdam lake IJ and 'BE' for the capital of Belgium. Buildings in the form of letters often denote a place and are positioned in the urban landscape so they are legible from a distance.

In form and meaning, these letter buildings refer back to the famous *Hollywood* sign in Los Angeles. Once intended to promote the sale of local property, this sign has now been given a permanent place as a landmark in the cityscape and symbolizes the film industry that flourishes here with all its glitz and glamor.

Recently, the Danish architectural firm Bay Arch proposed transforming the somewhat dilapidated sign into a hotel, with letters twice as big as they now are. In their proposal, the maintenance of the sign would be guaranteed and the sign would become accessible to the public. Moreover, the views from the rooms in the proposed hotel would be spectacular. That is the advantage of a highly visible location.

Besides creating a landmark, a letter or letter combination can also explain the function of a building. The Chinese character for people, Ren, befits a building for the people. The Stichting IK (I Foundation) has established its headquarters in a building complex shaped like the letters 'IK.' And in Dubai, the vision of Emir Maktoum bin Rashid Al Maktoum will be immortalized in a series of floating islands that spell out an Arabic poem.

Not all letter buildings form a word and have a real meaning though. The 'T' buildings in Copenhagen, the '#' building' in Seoul, the '*' building in Beijing or the 'W' building in Prague all derived their shapes from practical considerations. For example, a 'T' shape provides space for many apartments at the top with views, while a 'W' shape provides larger floor plans for offices on the first couple of floors and smaller ones for the apartments above. The coincidental meaning of the found object can be developed further in the marketing of the project and the experience of the public. Ultimately, a letter remains a letter.

An interesting aspect is that designs for letter-shaped buildings, in the form of both vertical and horizontal letters, were already made in the seventeenth and eighteenth century. At that time, buildings were designed for every letter of the alphabet. However, these designs were intended only as thought experiments. With the current designs, that is different: these designs are ready to be built.

Asterisk winery near Beijing by SAKO Architects (2010-2013)

Cross # Towers in Seoul by BIG (2012)

People's Building in Shanghai by BIG and JDS (2004)

Walter Tower in Prague by BIG (2007)

Y office building in Amsterdam by NL Architects (1999)

Masterplan Vejle Harbour, Denmark, by BIG and JDS (2003)

Hollywood Sign Hotel in Los Angeles by Bay Arch (2010)

T-Husene in Copenhagen by Steven Holl Architects (2006)

Poem as part of Palm Jebel Ali in Dubai by Waterstudio.NL (from 2002 onwards)

Housing in Hoek van Holland, the Netherlands, by MVRDV (2005)

IK paviljoen (I pavilion) in Oost-Souburg, the Netherlands, by Jan van Munster (2011)

Interview
Adriaan Geuze

'Ornament is everywhere, it is part of our DNA'

Jubilee Gardens in London by West 8 (competition phase, 2005)

Adriaan Geuze (1960) is a Dutch landscape architect. Together with Edzo Bindels and Martin Biewenga, he is a managing director of West 8 Urban Design & Landscape Architecture. Adriaan Geuze was curator of the second International Architecture Biennial Rotterdam in 2005, which was titled *The Flood*. In addition to the main location in Rotterdam, West 8 also has an office in New York.

The interview with Adriaan Geuze is held in the West 8 office in Rotterdam with a panoramic view of the Meuse River and the port of Rotterdam.

One of the many projects West 8 has worked on in recent years is the design of the Jubilee Gardens. In 2005, the architecture office won

Cliff-like border of the Jubilee Gardens (competition phase, 2005)

Schouwburgplein in Rotterdam by West 8 (1991-1996)

the competition for this park in the center of London with a design in which landscape architecture transitions into architecture. The rolling grass landscape that West 8 proposed for the park would be cut off sharply on its edges – very similar to how the rolling British landscape is sharply cut off at the coast by the white chalk cliffs of the Seven Sisters. To reinforce this reference, West 8 designed white panels with a limestone relief for the edge of the park landscape in London. With respect to material, the office came up with the idea of using low-maintenance polyester concrete. Because this material is easily shaped, it was possible to integrate benches and other park facilities into the panels. At the location where the polyester concrete wall was highest, West 8 proposed integrating a shop, a restaurant or an information center into the wall. For the lawn areas in the park, the office wanted to select the best grass variety in all of Great Britain – a country renowned for its grasses. On the lawn areas, West 8 designed lampposts in the shape of giant golf clubs.

During the first decade of the present century, a number of architects began experimenting in their designs with figurative ornament at the scale of the building. In several of your park designs, such as your design for the Jubilee Gardens in London, I see a comparable use of ornament. Can you identify with that?

'In our work, references and illusions play an important role. We are not averse to ornament. But it must serve a purpose. Also for visual appearance. We don't use ornament everywhere, as happened in the Rococo style, but we use it for accents.

In one of our first projects, the design for Schouwburgplein in Rotterdam, we made a "poem" to the port. We gave the movable lampposts the color of the Willemsbrug, the nearby bridge. In the paving,

the materials from the port return: granite, wood, steel. At dusk this provides a certain surrealistic feeling.

This is simply a very old-fashioned approach to the craft. Landscape architecture, or garden design, is all about providing illusion. That's what matters. It has nothing to do with ornament, ornament is something else.'

How do you define ornament?

'Ornament begins when you take a step beyond the strictly functional. When the eye is drawn to something, that's ornament. In the Kunsthal, Rem Koolhaas equipped a tension rod – from which a balcony is suspended – with an off-size screw. That is ornament as well. And I think that ornament is very important for homo sapiens. You see it in jewelry and on dresses. Ornament is everywhere.'

Nevertheless, ornament was taboo for many years.

'In postwar landscape architecture, ornament played virtually no role. Our work, however, connects with a different tradition. I believe

Governors Island in New York Harbor by West 8 (from 2007 onwards)

Wilhelminahof in Rotterdam by West 8 (2007)

that landscape architecture and storytelling belong together. Ornaments play a role in this process. As long as they remain subtle, you can tell more stories with them. But if it is too literal, the story becomes diluted.'

In your work, the ornament is sometimes more abstract and sometimes more literal. How do you make this choice?

'I don't have an answer to that question. We almost always keep the ornament abstract. However, there are a few designs which I think could have been even more abstract.'

Can you give an example?

'In the design for Wilhelminahof in Rotterdam, we applied a pattern of oak leaves to the glass plates, because there are oak trees in that courtyard. That is just too easy. It reminds everyone of oak leaves.'

If it is too simple, some of the illusion is lost?

'The ornament in Wilhelminahof has a function. It prevents you from walking into the glass. But it is not a subtle ornament.'

On the other hand, an overly abstract ornament doesn't work either; the public then no longer recognizes the reference. How do you view the tension between these extremes?

'In Greek architecture you often see motifs that are derived from plants or animals. Sometimes the ornament has a referential meaning, which is the case with the lions that guard Nelson's column on Trafalgar Square in London. In a philosophical sense, the Acanthus leaf in the capital of a Corinthian column perhaps refers to living nature. But this

has become such a cliché that it can hardly be called a literal reference. Why do women wear dresses with images of flowers? Could the motifs refer to nature? If you ask women about this, they would tell you that they simply want to look pretty.'

So the references in your work should not be taken literally?

'Of course they should. For example, in landscape architecture we work on parks in which we use ornament to refer, not coincidentally, to a different nature.'

And when designing a park or a square, can you deliberately refer to the port?

'Yes. At Governors Island, just off the coast of New York City, we thought it would be interesting if the park referred to the sea, so it would become more of an island.'

How do you accomplish that in your design?

'For the island, we designed bicycles with wooden frames in the shape of a hybrid bird's head, an amalgamation of the heads of an sea eagle, a goose and a duck. We also designed patterns in the paving and the railings referring to the world of coral and seaweed. It does not become too obvious, but it does have a relationship with these elements.'

Is it your intention that the public recognizes these references?

'You can see them, but you don't need to. The references are successful because they are subtle. It is no Walt Disney.'

What do you mean by Walt Disney? That the reference becomes too literal? It then becomes kitsch?

'If the flower motif on a Greek column should literally become a flower, then it no longer works. If you look properly, and you are familiar with botany, then you would recognize a grape leaf. While a layman only thinks: that is some kind of floral motif. And someone who walks past the column every day no longer sees the floral motif at all. They would only see the effect of the shadows, and that it holds a bird's nest. That is a good ornament. That it is part of everyday life, but that – if you want to – you can see more in it.

The buildings in Art Deco style are full of such ornaments. And they all refer to flowers. For that matter, the discovery of Tutankhamen's tomb gave an impulse to Art Deco too. It also comprised the mystery of antiquity.

I think that landscape architecture and garden art were all about the ornament. If you read about gardens from the Middle Ages, Islamic gardens, baroque gardens, our own landscape tradition . . . they are all about style, about the position and about the ground plan. But I really think – and I have studied them – that all these gardens are also permanent illusions of life and death, that they are about perversion, power, desire, love, monsters, ghosts, dragons, heaven and hell, violence, being gay. All gardens are about this and in the course of history nothing, and I mean nothing, has changed. This is a continuous line.

It's in the position of the water, in the reflection, in the Hercules statues. Very many gardens, you can't get around it, are an exposé of homosexuality and violence. It is almost impossible not to see this. For me, this is very evident. I think that garden design has carried these references with it for a very long time. Garden design has access to an enormous palette of ornamentation. And this ornamentation has been developed to the point that it has become an art in itself. That is why we think railings, fences, edging details, and similar aspects are so beautiful. Because it gives the eye something to do.

The transition from classical to modern architecture is fascinating; to me it is an example of the balance between spatial art and ornamentation. Mies van der Rohe designed ornaments with his chromed square columns and with his folded natural stones. He had still been trained to design with ornament. There are always edges that attract the eye. And if you look closely, you also see this in the work of Rem Koolhaas. But it is subtle, many people do not see it.

In landscape architecture, ornament disappeared long ago. Now it is only about straight lines, about railings with wrought iron fences, lanterns without curves. Even the trees are perfectly straight now.'

You were trained as a landscape architect at Wageningen University. Were stories like this about the ornamentation of gardens told there?

Oosterschelde Storm Surge Barrier, the Netherlands, by West 8 (1990-1992)

Bridge in the Noorderpark

Noorderpark in Amsterdam by West 8 (from 2003 onwards)

'Everywhere in the world, the story of garden design is told as a story about the layout of the garden. I have no memory of the literature going into ornamentation.'

What made you decide to delve into this?

'When I was studying, I read Tom Wolfe. That certainly played a role.

We used ornament in the very first design our office made. At the Oosterschelde storm surge barrier in the Dutch province of Zeeland, we were asked to design the landscape elements for the former workplaces of the buttress dam. Our clients at Rijkswaterstaat (Department of Public Works) were primarily ecologists. The question I wanted to ask with the design was whether an ecological design could be devoid of shape or reference. We made a striped pattern with white and black sea shells. On these two backgrounds, two colors of birds could make their nests. Possibly, in that way, you could organize nature. That was the statement. In the orderly Dutch landscape, nature is also orderly. Even the frogs are put in straight lines. It goes that far. In this design, we suggested that birds would rest in straight lines at high tide. As a result, the design has ornamental power. This aspect is part of our entire oeuvre. That has remained the same.

In the design for the Oosterschelde storm surge barrier, however, the ornament is more than a reference, it is also an experience. When you're driving your car at 100 kilometers per hour past the striped pattern, you experience the rhythm of it. It's almost like music. The alternating stripes amplify the perspective of the emptiness.

In the Noorderpark in Amsterdam, we recently designed a leaf pattern derived from the ivy that is abundant there. We transferred that leaf pattern to the asphalt to indicate the zones for pedestrians and cyclists. It is also very interesting to me how an ornament such as this can be translated into a contemporary texture.'

By using contemporary technology?

'Yes. In the Noorderpark, we also developed a cast aluminum fence in which the same leaf pattern is repeated. It is almost Rococo in appearance.'

In architecture the ornament sometimes refers to the function of the building and sometimes to its context. When designing a park, these two quickly coincide. In the Noorderpark the ornament refers to the design of the park and to the immediate context of the paths and fences.

'You search for a recognizable visual language for the park.'

So that you define a place?

'You must use ornament consistently. If it does not have a context, it quickly becomes uninteresting.'

In your design for the Toronto Waterfront, you drew an island in the shape of a Maple leaf, the national symbol of Canada. The context to

Toronto Waterfront by West 8 (from 2006 onwards)

which the ornament refers then becomes huge in scale: a country.

'That is a rather unfortunate example. The design for the Toronto Waterfront was part of a competition. You have to imagine that process. You have to make your point clear, not only to a jury, but also to the general public. As part of this, you stage an act. However, I don't mean to say that this is all you have to do. You must have a good plan, stay within budget and present points of which the client thinks: these are my points. Moreover, in a democratic city like Toronto, you have to get the public vote. Without the latter, the Mayor is not going to support your plan.'

To appeal to that general public, do you look for a catchy image?

'No, no. We noted that the Toronto Waterfront lacked an identity. We asked ourselves whether all the elements that a Canadian has in his cottage on a lake during the weekend could be brought to this metropolis.

Profile of the Simcoe Wavedeck at the Toronto Waterfront

A foreground of trees, a shore of wood, a few deck chairs and a boot. To realize this, we first made a plan based on the root space required for new maple and elm trees. These were never planted before. Then we proposed detailing everything in granite and wood. Everything.

A second factor that played a role was that the Toronto waterfront was very lacking in natural aspects, therefore its redevelopment should have a positive impact on their recovery. The polluted soil of the lakebed will be remediated. Approximately $40 million has already been spent on capturing rainwater, so that it no longer flows directly into the lake. Moreover, new shallow areas have been created. Because the harbor is relatively deep, we proposed using mesh to create a large shallow area, so that a new microenvironment could develop.

You can present that story, but not like a picture in the newspaper. We therefore decided to relate the ecological program to the biggest attraction on the water, the highest tower in North America: the CN Tower. We positioned the shallow area along the axis of that tower. For its shape, we bombastically used the cliché figure of the Maple Leaf, knowing that if we won the competition, that the Maple Leaf would be finished. We were not concerned with the image itself, but with the program behind the image.

Street light at the Toronto Waterfront

Why does Lady Gaga wear a dress made out of meat? Because she wants to promote the consumption of meat? Because she wants to show how concerned she is about animal welfare? Or simply because she wants to be in the picture? You can tell all these stories, but in reality the latter reason applies to her.'

Of course.

'That was the design competition, and look at what is now being realized. For the quay we made wooden bridges. The bridges are supported by wooden columns, and where they come together, we designed a sort of hand, a steel ornament. In this ornament you can recognize the abstraction of a Maple Leaf. The balusters of the cast iron benches on the wooden deck have a relief on which, in certain light conditions, you can also recognize an abstraction of the Maple Leaf. These are the ornaments.

On the quay there are also wooden lampposts. In the steel base of the posts, a print of tree bark can be seen. It is the bark of the Blue Pine, the same tree used for the wood of the lampposts. However, this ornament is more than a subtle reference. The base of a lamppost can also become very discolored. Because it is now very rough, it will only acquire more patina as it discolors. The ornament must also serve a purpose. It must solve a construction problem or turn discoloration into a positive quality.'

It really has a function.

'Yes it does. And that Maple leaf in the lake . . . we needed a vehicle to make our story clear. You have to imagine that we had only 10 minutes to provide something of value to a room of 500 people. That is an art in itself. You want them to understand the message and remember something of what you have drawn. With that image, we explained the ecological program very successfully. I said that it could even have the shape of a Maple Leaf. At that point, people laughed. And then you know right away that the city council and the Mayor will accept the plan, but will ask you to forget the leaf. You feel that immediately.'

Mixed use of the Simcoe Wavedeck at the Toronto Waterfront

So really, the image of the Maple Leaf was a kind of ornament for the presentation.

'Yes.'

To finish the story: what is the background of the Wave Decks?

'In Toronto, it gets just as cold as in Chicago. For much of the year it is very windy. The street pattern of Toronto is a grid, which ends very abruptly at the lake. Skyscrapers are located along the waterfront and there is a sort of motorway with concrete sidewalks and a concrete tram line. Truly ruthless. In that urban canyon you do not have any sense of where Lake Ontario is. At the end of every street leading to the lake is a slip-end. Our proposal was to provide a deck above the water at all these slip-ends.

With these decks, we wanted to express the investments that have been made to improve the quality of the water and the soil. That a kind of euphoria about this would emerge. At each slip-end we allowed the boardwalk to undulate, and in this way to give each slip-end its own silhouette. This also creates a reason to sit down. One wave bends down so you can lounge near the canoes. Another wave bends up and forms a small amphitheater. And yet another wave is hardly a wave at all, but it does resolve three height differences.

If you see it all together, the boardwalk is a sort of music that transcends everyday experience. A plain wooden deck is a wooden deck and no more than that. With an undulating wooden deck, however, you wonder what it is. It makes you want to walk on it.

The boardwalk was an immediate success because the wooden decks remind the Canadians of . . . the dock on the lake at their holiday home where they spend the weekend. But it is not exactly that association, because the deck undulates. However, it is still this association that gives the waterfront for this city of 5 million people that extra bit of support, and makes the waterfront something more of a waterfront. It has been made livable for ordinary people. It is an avant-garde story.'

Thinker on a Rock-sculpture on the Neude square in Utrecht, the Netherlands, by artist Barry Flanagan (2002)

Exactly, everyone can go along with it.

'And if you look closely, you can see that we have worked very hard on the detailing of the quay. The ornament is mainly there. The planks are all slightly tilted to prevent people from slipping on the wooden wave decks. This creates a saw tooth pattern that gives you much more traction. That sort of thing. It is a bold design. Your eye is drawn to all kinds of details.

We did the same thing at Schouwburgplein. It appears to be a simple, empty square, but as soon as you step onto the square you discover that the planks are laid to form a fishbone motif. The surfaces seem to be inclined. That is the added ornamentality.'

The ornaments in your designs, how do they relate to the visual arts? Do you work together with artists when making the design? Or do you design them yourselves?

'We work together with artists in every project. But in most cases, this leads to autonomous art. In our design for Wilhelminahof in Rotterdam, for example, we requested the placement of a large sculpture that refers to the nearby oil refineries of Pernis.

For the Neude square in Utrecht, we had the idea that a classical, bronze sculpture was required. Six streets come together at the square. The situation is comparable to 19th-century squares in cities like Berlin or Vienna. For this location, the sculptor Barry Flanagan designed a thinking hare on a pedestal.

In Lelystad, we designed a parking garage with a 300 meter long painting by an Amsterdam artist. The painting is printed onto the glass panels of the façade of the building. The biggest challenge there was to obtain sufficient support and funding for this artwork.

These works of art reach a fairly high level. In Madrid, we designed two concrete vaulted pedestrian bridges. We wanted the bridges to become a meeting place, where you wouldn't have the feeling of standing on the bridge, but inside the bridge. Together with the director of the Prado Museum, we selected an artist, a well-known photographer, to work on the inside of the bridges. He photographed residents who lived near the bridges. Their portraits are presented in the vaulted ceilings of the bridge.

We introduced the artist to the Spanish ceramics industry. Using a computer, he abstracted the artwork to pixels, to form a pattern of millions of tiles. These tiles were then manually installed on the vaulted ceilings. The artwork has become so popular that the bridges are no longer our bridges, but the bridges of the artist.

For that matter, the bridges themselves also have ornaments. For example, the deck of the bridge narrows and widens, there are constructive details and the bridges are equipped with beautiful railings.'

So you do not commission any artists for the ornaments in your work?

'I do not know why I would ask an artist to do a pavement pattern or baluster. Most contemporary artists don't do that kind of work anyway. They celebrate their autonomy. However, I see that an ornament sometimes yields something in the world of design or the world of art; it sometimes goes beyond what we as landscape architects are capable of doing.'

Looking towards the future, do you expect any changes in how you design ornaments?

'The ornament is important for homo sapiens. It is not only part of architecture or landscape architecture, it is everywhere. In clothing and tattoos. But also on wallpaper, draperies and furniture. The era determines which color and which design are fashionable. In the 1950s, everything was somewhat rounded, so that the eye could always rest on something. Ornament is also present in very plain architecture. In that case, for example, it is an edge. The ornament is timeless, it is part of our DNA. This will not change in the future.

We are always searching for explicit ornament, which hopefully

Interior of one of the Puentes Cascara

Puentes Cascara in Madrid by West 8 (2006-2011)

112

Avenida de Portugal in Madrid by West 8 (2006-2011)

refers to something, which is capable of strengthening the design and ordering the context, or which is alienating.

Our office was once asked to design a park under a number of railway viaducts in Amsterdam Sloterdijk. But there was no daylight, so how could we make a park there? So we made Cor-Ten steel tree trunks with artificial light inside that projected tree rings on the viaducts above. You make quite a statement with such a design, a big exclamation mark. Just like Madonna – very deliberately – placed a mole above her lip.'

Every time you study the location.

'Yes. Bilbao was a dirty, old, stinking city on a river, with a steel industry and the memories of hard-working, hard-headed Basques. A city in decline, desperate for a Renaissance. At that location, you build a Guggenheim Museum designed by Frank Gehry. This is an appeal to a new world. A heaven on earth. A world in which buildings can melt, move, flutter like fire . . . . It is an exaggerated building, but rightly so. I do not think that we should design all buildings in this way, but it fits with this location.'

Carrascoplein in Amsterdam by West 8 (1998)

Interview
Michiel Riedijk

Lake side housing The Sphinxes in Huizen, the Netherlands, by Neutelings Riedijk Architects (1996-2003)

'It is all about a cultural signification that communicates what is happening inside a building'

Michiel Riedijk (1964) is a Dutch architect. Together with Willem Jan Neutelings, he is a managing director of Neutelings Riedijk Architects. Since 2007, Riedijk has been Professor of Architectural Design at Delft University of Technology (TU Delft).

I meet with Riedijk at his office in Rotterdam. During the interview he draws the floor plans and cross sections of the projects we discuss on a roll of tracing paper.

From the moment that you started your firm, in your work the ornament at the scale of the building seems to have become more literal. Has it?

'I don't recognize that image immediately. In the first design of our firm, the Minnaert Building, you can already discern multiple layers that you could call ornamental. In our designs, we always aim to differentiate three levels of intervention. You can't really see them separately from each other.

The first level, of course, is that of the primary shape. The urban silhouette, the way the building is molded against the sky and the way the program is brought together into a single sculpture. In some cases, such as the Scheepvaart en Transport College (STC) in Rotterdam or the Sphinxes in Huizen, the primary shape can have a narrative side. However, for us that is never a goal in itself. It is sometimes more of a coincidence than a deliberate intention during the design process.

The second level of intervention, after the primary shape, is the composition of the windows and other elements that must appear in the face of the façade. This involves the façade as a space or zone that mediates between inside and outside. This is the level at which frames, glasses, edges, seams and the like are formed, which dramatize the transition between inside and outside. The depth of the openings for the windows, the window sills and the setbacks also play a role here. This is actually found in all our work: both in our more anthropomorphic, narrative work and in the more abstract volumes.

The third level concerns the materiality and tactility of the building. This is the intervention at the detail level of the material. At that level, you see a wide range of experiments in our projects, from the dragons of Tirza that we designed for the Tax Office in Apeldoorn, to the glass panels that we made together with Jaap Drupsteen for the Netherlands Institute for Sound and Vision in Hilversum.

Each design that we make intervenes at these three levels. I therefore find it difficult to isolate a single level and discuss it exclusively. They are all linked together. However, having said that, I do think that a number of our buildings could be called a Duck, in the Venturian sense of the word, where the primary shape expresses what is happening in the building. There are also buildings that can be read as a Decorated Shed, also in the Venturian sense of the word, with a relatively neutral, box-like primary shape that is provided with an iconographic or decorative layer of signification.'

Minnaert Building in Utrecht, the Netherlands, by Neutelings Riedijk Architects (1994-1997)

Post Office in Zichem, Belgium, by Neutelings Riedijk Architects (1994-1997)

Netherlands Institute for Sound and Vision in Hilversum, the Netherlands, by Neutelings Riedijk Architects (1999-2006)

Let's zoom in on a project to make the story more concrete. For example, how did you arrive at the design for the Sphinx apartment buildings in Huizen? You designed the project as early as in 1995, didn't you?

'The Sphinx apartment buildings were completed in 2002. In 1995 we were working on the Minnaert Building in Utrecht, the Sphinxes in Huizen and the Post Office in Zichem. If I look at the narrative layer in the work of our office, that is not something that began with the Sphinxes. This could just as well apply to the Minnaert Building and the Post Office. The only difference is that in the Sphinxes, it is perhaps somewhat more explicit.

The earth color and texture of the shotcrete, and the grooves in the façade of the Minnaert Building form a narrative, an analogy that says something about the faculties of Earth Sciences, Geophysics and Physics that were to be accommodated in the building. The relatively long, very unusual volume arose simply because the building had to make a connection with two other buildings.

The concrete sand dune with glass skylights, where pilgrims in Zichem can mail their postcards, says something about how the Virgin Mary appeared in the village as a luminous figure on a sand dune. The sand dune is an extension of a historical building, which also accommodates part of the post office.'

Are the Sphinxes in Huizen also an expression of the program?

'No, not entirely. In Huizen, we had already designed homes on the waterfront. Subsequently, we were asked to design the waterfront itself, and then homes that had to be built in the water. To maximize the views from the waterfront onto the water, we wanted the perspective to become open (to represent the buildings in the water, Riedijk draws a tapered volume). At the same time, we wanted each residence to have a view of the water and to have a very private terrace on the south. Because the waterfront is on the north, the solution was a volume that angles towards the waterfront. In this way, each apartment also has a view back towards the waterfront. Finally, in order to give the rearmost apartments, which were located farthest from the waterfront, a south-facing balcony with a view, we decided to broaden that part of the building (Riedijk draws another, smaller, tapered volume, a mirror image, over the first one). Consequently, the primary shape of the building is the result of a fairly straightforward logic based on orientation towards the sun, the view of the water and the view from and towards the waterfront.'

So it is simply very functional.

'Yes. After we decided on the logic of this approach and discovered the shape that emerged from stacking the apartments in this way, we amplified the theme with the addition of intermediate-scale elements such as balconies, frames and glasses. In this way, the *Gestalt* of the primary shape was strengthened. On the one hand, the primary shape

Lake side housing The Sphinxes

emanates from the location, but on the other hand, at a certain moment there is also a longing or obsession with shape that underlies its articulation.'

Because you could have also attempted to deny the shape that emerged?

'Yes.'

So you wanted to use this shape here. How did your client respond?

'Well, at first we only used the metaphor internally to discuss the shape amongst ourselves. However, at a certain point we externalized the metaphor, and the client embraced the idea. The metaphor ultimately became part of their sales strategy. They used the name Sphinxes to sell the project, to brand it – to use that awful word. But there is always a certain point in time when you are vulnerable to how the client is going to respond to something like this.'

TWA Flight Center on John F. Kennedy International Airport in New York by Eero Saarinen (1956-1962)

About 10 years later, there are architects, such as Alejandro Zaero-Polo, who use the metaphors that they find to actually sell the design to the client and the general public. What is your view on this practice?

'Metaphors are complicated. There are a few famous metaphorical buildings, such as the TWA Terminal by Eero Saarinen. This project is supported by the metaphor of wings or flying. However, the primary shape of the terminal, with the wings and the branching piers, makes the design incredibly constrained. Consequently, the metaphor also makes the design vulnerable. The metaphor probably worked well in communicating the project to the client, but on the other hand, you see that having to maintain the metaphor didn't do the project any good. Therefore we do not actually communicate the metaphor to a client ourselves.'

So as an architect, it is better not to tell this?

'Indeed. You run the risk that the chosen primary shape will become more of an obstacle than a help. The design for the TWA Terminal clearly shows the vulnerability of this strategy.'

By not communicating the metaphor, you are endeavoring to maintain your freedom of design? Or does the desire to keep the metaphor abstract also play a role?

'Both. We are always seeking abstraction. First of all, we seek abstraction in the assignment itself. We want to understand the assignment based on parameters that are almost mathematical. In addition, we try to avoid discussions with the client about metaphors and appearance. Otherwise, the design process becomes extremely vulnerable.'

You try to objectify the design?

'Yes, you try to come up with objective criteria with which you can discuss the quality of the design.'

So you use fact-based arguments instead of discussions focusing on topics such as the exact color of the façade?

'By using the metaphor as a strategy, you can get yourself cornered. At a certain point, you are no longer capable of identifying the strength or weakness of the metaphorical layer.'
That sounds like a strong warning to everyone who works with metaphors.

When your firm discusses sculptures and writes about them, you address topics such as orbitals, crests and the like. In that case, you compare a building with the human figure.

'It was Alberti who introduced the comparison with the human body into the architectural debate of the Renaissance. For Alberti, this comparison was always linked to the notion of completeness: there is left and right, top and bottom, in front of and behind. Generally speaking, in the architectural debate, besides the notion of completeness, the comparison with the human figure is often used to arrive at the correct proportions. In both cases, the human figure represents the divine.

In our work, the anthropomorphic comparison has to do with the composition of the volume. Referring to glasses, head, tail, edge, collar, crest and the like defines the relationship of one part to another part. In that sense, we are perhaps truly Renaissance architects. The crest is in proportion to the head, the glasses are in proportion to the nose, and the torso is in proportion to the legs. The relationship between a large glass window with a surrounding edge and the room behind it can best be described as a building wearing glasses.'

Another point: during your study of architecture, did you focus on Postmodernism?

'For me, James Stirling and Robert Venturi were really important. One of the first field trips that I took as an architecture student in the 1980s was to the museum that Stirling had designed in Stuttgart. I still admire the intelligent way in which the museum is integrated into the urban landscape, how routes through the city and routes through the building are superimposed. We organized our design for the STUC in Leuven in a comparable fashion. In the design we had to deal with the same height difference as Stirling did in Stuttgart. I learned that meticulous urban integration from Postmodernism. Stirling however has never been a style icon for me.

Robert Venturi is probably just as important. From Venturi I learned about the power you can acquire from precedents; the unscrupulous use of intelligence that can be found in other buildings. In that respect, the Venturi who wrote *Complexity and Contradiction* is more influential than the Venturi who wrote *Learning from Las Vegas*.'

The latter probably applies to most architects.

'Postmodernism is part of the genetic composition of our office. But at the same time it isn't, in the sense that Rem Koolhaas and Aldo Rossi are equally important. They could also be classified as post-modernists, but for us they represent another side of architecture.'

And Frank Gehry? Did you look at his work during your studies?

'No, not really. There are interesting elements in the early work of Gehry, such as the instrument of enlargement and reduction. In the design of the office for Chiat/Day in Los Angeles, for example, Gehry placed large binoculars by artist Claes Oldenburg in front of the building, resulting in a crazy leap of scale. Very interesting, but not worthy of following.'

Similar to your firm, Gehry approached his designs as sculptures.

'Yes, but the work of Gehry is very personal, it is almost autobiographical. The architecture of Stirling and Venturi is easier to explain and is consequently more accessible.'

We have now discussed the start-up phase of your office and the projects

Museum aan de Stroom (MAS) in Antwerp by Neutelings Riedijk Architects (2000-2010)

Canteen of the Shipping and Transport College

Shipping and Transport College in Rotterdam by Neutelings Riedijk Architects (2001-2006)

you worked on at that time. How has ornament developed itself in your work since then?

'I don't know if anything has really changed in the thinking of our office. However, I do believe that our skill as architects has improved. We have become more aware of the levels of intervention that we can utilize. Consequently, you see that that our interventions at various levels of scale have become increasingly rich. We have certainly developed ourselves in that regard.'

You have gained experience.

'Yes. It is actually very simple.'

Projects that your firm currently delivers have sometimes been designed a few years ago, but in the case of the Museum aan de Stroom (MAS), the design was completed more than a decade ago. Consequently, the development of your work is not easy to assess.

'You cannot simply read the work chronologically. You have to be cautious with that, because over time interferences between projects can occur.

When we designed the Sphinxes in 1995, it was materialized in green wooden plates. This can be seen in the *El Croquis* bookazine about our firm in 1999. Based on our experiences with other projects, we discovered that it would be better to build this project in aluminum. That is how it was built in 2002.

The MAS was designed in 1999. In that respect, it is an old piece of work. But because it was completed between 2006 and 2009, we were able to incorporate what we learned from the Shipping and Transport College in Rotterdam and the Netherlands Institute for Sound and Vision in Hilversum.

So chronology is difficult. I think that we have become increasingly precise in what a building should communicate. How a building gives shape to the public domain. At the level of decoration, we are applying an ever-stronger narrative layer, such as the hands at the MAS in Antwerp or the dragons at the Tax Office in Apeldoorn.

I think this is an interesting development in our work. It is not about decoration as such, but about the fact that we believe that a building gives shape to the public domain. And that public domain cannot be shaped with offices on a standard grid of 7.20 m. It is also about offering stories and landmarks in the urban landscape, which in turn can create new stories.'

Should everyone be able to understand this ornament?

'Well, our work has many layers. There is an intellectual layer, which has to do with our training and our position in the field of architecture. But there is also a very immediate layer that has to do with visual culture, comic books, pop art and television culture. By the way, in these various layers we don't try to create a hierarchy.'

The primary shape of the Shipping and Transport College on the Lloyd pier in Rotterdam refers to port cranes and stacked shipping containers. Can you explain how this design came about?

'For the Shipping and Transport College, we didn't want the expression of a school, because it's more than that, and we also didn't want the expression of an office building, because it isn't that either. It is an institute for maritime affairs, that also wanted to provide a place in its building for all kinds of equipment with which maritime situations can be simulated. Consequently, we wanted to create an object that would join the port landscape. The building had to be family of the cranes, silos and warehouses that you find in the port. These often have strange shapes and large cantilevers. That is where we based the iconography of the Shipping and Transport College on.'

The ornaments in your design refer to objects outside architecture. The interior of the Shipping and Transport College has ceilings like sails, doors are equipped with portholes and the lecture hall on the top floor is equipped with square "life vests". Has the set of instruments of the architect expanded in the course of history?

'No, I don't think so. The instruments are the same as they always were. Only the themes have changed. As an architect, you can be inspired by anything. The ancient Greeks found inspiration for their ornament in the Acanthus leaf. Nowadays you look at different things. A contemporary writer uses the same grammar as a writer from a century ago, but writes books on different themes. After all, other matters have now become important.'

Other architects sometimes complain that the ornament in your designs occasionally becomes too literal.

'I agree. That is our lack of talent. It is important to have layers of meaning. Things that have only a single meaning, whether it's a book or a building, quickly become boring. While things that are richer in meaning remain interesting for a longer period of time.

It is true that some of our buildings are rather flat and that we did not succeed in realizing the layeredness. Sometimes this is because the assignment was too limited, but sometimes it is simply because we were unable to do better. That's just the way it is.

The funny thing is that buildings with many layers, such as the Tax Office in Apeldoorn, remain hermetic and elusive for many people, while a quickly understand-

Gargouilles ligning the entrance to the Dutch Tax Office, Walterbos Complex

Dutch Tax Office, Walterbos Complex, in Apeldoorn, the Netherlands, by Neutelings Riedijk Architects (2001-2007)

able shape is absorbed more quickly into contemporary visual culture. Which is not to say that that is better. But it varies with the building. For example, you can find more layers of signification at the Netherlands Institute for Sound and Vision in Hilversum than at the Shipping and Transport College in Rotterdam.'

For the Tax Office in Apeldoorn, you designed an ornament in the shape of a dragon. How did you come up with that design? How did the users of that building complex respond to this ornament?

'Actually, we have received hardly any reactions from the users.'

But the client was enthusiastic?

'Yes. But you have to see it in its context. We construed the Walter Bos complex of the Tax Office in Apeldoorn as a castle. The client understood this analogy. The dragons are part of that story.

With the design for the Tax Office, we experienced a sort of inverse process. On the building site, everything had already been determined. There were office towers from the 1970s, new office towers designed by the architecture firm DP6 and various buildings with computer facilities. We were given the assignment to make a whole out of this ensemble.

To accomplish this, we first put the ground surface under water. In this water feature we excavated sunken gardens, partly from existing basements. Around the gardens we built covered corridors to access the surrounding buildings and connect them to each other. To provide the world around the sunken gardens with daylight, above the water feature we created a field with daylight collectors.

The building complex can also literally be seen as a castle, with its closed inner courtyard, large water features and spouting gargoyles that escort the users of the building to its main entrance.

In these buildings, the tax revenues from the Netherlands are counted. It is a kind of digital Fort Knox. Our client, the Government Buildings Agency, understood the castle analogy completely. And a castle is guarded by monsters: dragons and water-spouting giants. From the actual user, the Tax Office, we didn't really receive any feedback.'

So you did use the ornament here to make the client more enthusiastic about your design?

'No. For us it was a way to increase the abstraction. At this location, so much architecture was already present that we thought: we should make something very abstract that in its language of shape and its materialization is not part of any of the existing architecture. The stainless steel skylights backed away from the existing imagery on the site. The masks and dragons that were stamped into the steel amplified that effect.

For us it was more about the architectural composition than finding a metaphor with which the client could be seduced. The client was most impressed by the fact that with this design we could connect all the buildings and that the whole site could be returned to the public domain. A publicly accessible route now runs through the previously closed site. The park at the rear of the site has been returned to the city.'

So once again, very functional considerations were involved?

'Yes, we made very practical arguments with which the community living around the complex could be persuaded. With our design we were able to eliminate much of the resistance to the project. Simply because we did a lot for the neighborhood. We also took the cars off the street. With such interventions, the location of such a building complex in a residential district becomes self-evident again.'

At which point in this process did you say: we add the dragons?

'Fairly early in the process. For us, the dragons were part of the intervention at the level of materiality. Fairly early in the process we had the idea of fabricating the light collectors from stainless steel, simply because it is one of the few materials that could be placed in the rainwater basins. At that point, we quickly looked at the production of stainless steel. An interesting property of stainless steel is that it can be worked so that it has a shape. We immediately had the idea of working with artists on this component. We did not yet know exactly what shape it would have. Ultimately, that became the dragons.'

Should the ornament always represent a virtue?

'The ornament has two sides. One side concerns craftsmanship, the making of the thing. On the other side, it must tell a story at the public level. What you call a virtue, I would like to rephrase to that it is about making a building that stands out from the background, from the residential buildings. We call that the "fond". You do that with an element that gives expression to what is happening in the building. And that doesn't have to be literal. For a maritime school, you do not have to place the word "Teaching" on the building, but you can refer to shipping containers, port facilities and periscopes. In this way it distinguishes itself from a residential accommodation and asks the question: what is the significance of the building in the public domain?'

In the nineteenth century, the representation of a building was linked to the function that it accommodated and to the social status of that function. A more important building had to be more richly ornamented, while the background was supposed to retreat. Do you follow this line?

'Absolutely. And it's not that public is more important than private. The point is that there is a separation between the private and the public domain, in which, let's say, the public has its own place. Sociologist Richard Sennett has noted that the public in our society is under pressure and is threatened by privatization. Everything has become an expression of a private desire. That which is still public can hardly be distinguished anymore.'

Indeed, you do see this confusion reflected in the architecture of some public buildings.

'Our residential buildings are therefore not decorated.'

Is that so? Didn't your office decide several years ago to not do any more residential buildings?

'We still designed a few residential buildings on the Müller pier in Rotterdam. The final building in this project has recently been delivered. These buildings are very modest and reserved.'

That's true. They are even repetitious.

'Yes. Although the buildings differ strongly in their typology, they can be seen as a family. They were designed as a background. And one of the characteristics of the background is repetition.'

In their work, other architects sometimes incorporate metaphors that are related to the context. Does your office do that as well?

'No. It is all about a cultural signification that communicates what is happening inside a building.'

By the end of the nineteenth century, ornament had become much cheaper to make and therefore there was a strong inflation of its significance. Anything could be ornamented. In the current era, once again you see this inflation and this confusion. Some residential buildings now are also richly ornamented.

'I see that as a misunderstanding.'

Blok 3 on the Müllerpier in Rotterdam by Neutelings Riedijk Architects (1999-2003)

Should architects restrain themselves? Or should monuments always take that extra step, always offer more shape?

'Architects should take a cultural position. And this position is about how you can provide significance to part of a city, a neighborhood or a building. Everything shouldn't look like a rental office building, but that also doesn't mean that everything should be heavily decorated. If no one takes a position, that will lead to homogeneity instead of quality.'

How do you expect ornament to develop in the work of your office in the future? Will you continue to use ornament at the small level of scale?

'Yes, I think so.'

The primary shape of your projects, such as the series of egg-shaped buildings that you designed, seems to have become more modest in the past years.

'The "eggs" that we designed for a casino in Knokke and a casino in Las Vegas were heavily decorative within the repetition of the façade. The nature of the primary shape does not influence the narrative at the middle scale and lower scale. In Paris, we designed a hotel in which a poem appears in the façade. In Arnhem we designed a building for several cultural institutions with large Penrose ornaments. The latter is an ornament consisting of an endlessly repeating pattern of diamond shapes. In this project it symbolizes the endless dispersion of knowledge.'

Rozet in Arnhem, the Netherlands, by Neutelings Riedijk Architects (2009-2013)

Interview
Alejandro Zaero-Polo

'The battle between iconography on one side and structure on the other side can be very productive'

Wave-like organisation of the Yokohama International Port Terminal (1995-2004)

Alejandro Zaero-Polo (1963) is a Spanish architect. Together with Maider Llaguno, he is director of the architectural firm AZPML (Alejandro Zaero-Polo Maider Llaguno Architecture), which has offices in London and Barcelona. He is also Dean of the School of Architecture at Princeton University.

AZPML is a continuation of FOA (Foreign Office Architects), which Zaero-Polo led with his wife Farshid Moussavi until their separation in 2011. All of the projects discussed in this interview were designed by FOA.

Ornament, including iconography, wasn't something Zaero-Polo worked on when he started out with FOA in 1993. His attention had been drawn to a new kind of architecture that favored complex, folded surfaces and glass screens. As the oeuvre of FOA shows, this type of architecture enabled all kinds of buildings to be 'folded': villas, office buildings, shopping malls, concert halls and train stations.

Within this pragmatic oeuvre, however, some projects stand out by also having an iconographic side. The Belgo restaurants designed by Foreign Office Architects are an early example of this. Their folded surfaces form contemporary brick barrel vaults to echo the atmosphere of an old Belgian cellar.

Belgo Zuid in London by Foreign Office Architects (1999)

The somewhat hidden strand of iconographic work from FOA developed after an event in February 1995. After winning the design competition for the Yokohama Cruise Terminal, Zaero-Polo and Moussavi were asked to present their design at a press conference at the Yokhohama City Hall. In his essay *The Hokusai Wave*, Zaero-Polo described the event as follows:

'Faithful to our doctrine, fine-tuned through years of academic practice, we proceeded to explain the circulation diagrams, the geometric transformations, and the construction technologies that were involved in the project, hoping that the audience would have enough patience to wait for the emergence of the project. Halfway through the presentation, we started to notice the blank expression of the public in the room – a clear indicator that the message was not coming across.

After a few minutes of cold sweat, an image that was carefully edited from the project's discourse but still floating somewhere in the back of our minds came suddenly to our rescue. It was the Hokusai

Wave, a drawing from a local painter that we had been toying with while we indulged in the geometric manipulations and construction hypotheses during the design phase of the competition entry.

In a sudden – and risky – burst of inspiration, we terminated the factual process narrative to conclude that what really inspired us was the image of Hokusai's Wave. The room exploded in an exclamation of sincere relief: "Aaaahhh...!" and we left the room, still sweating and grateful for the moment of lucidity, and with the clear realisation that something wasn't quite working on our carefully crafted discourse.'

Were you already thinking about iconography before the presentation of your design for the Yokohama International Port Terminal?

'I was thinking about it as something to avoid. I regarded it as a negative technique of doing architecture. Our position back then was a reaction to the fact that an earlier generation of architects had been interested in that, in metaphorical effects.'

So your interest in applying iconography in your work really emerged at that presentation?

'Yes, but at that moment it was just a pragmatic solution to a problem we had. I did, however, immediately realize how powerful the technique was and used it for a couple of years. Only later, I recognized that particular presentation as a sort of epiphany.'

After the presentation of the Yokohama International Port Terminal, Zaero-Polo started to develop a strategy that he now calls 'form with a double agenda'. In this strategy the proposed iconography is closely tied to the organization, the load-bearing structure and/or other technical aspects of the project. It's a coupling between iconography and material organization, as Zaero-Polo puts it.

With this strategy Zaero-Polo aims to create an iconography that runs deeper than just the skin of the building. The design for the Yokohama International Port Terminal is a good example of how this strategy works. The project not only looks like a wave: it has a wave-like organization and a wave-like construction too.

Was it the design for the Yokohama International Port Terminal that spurred the 'form with a double agenda' strategy? Or were there more projects in which you experienced a successful coupling of iconography and material organization?

'That strategy doesn't stem just from the Yokohama International Port Terminal, but from a series of projects.

Japan was a relatively straightforward place to work. As an architect you can be sincere. In Europe, where the politics are more complicated, you have to wear a mask all the time. When you enter the process of designing and realizing buildings or cities, you have to participate in local politics. You are drawn into it, whether you want to or not. To deal

Yokohama International Port Terminal, Japan, by Foreign Office Architects (1995-2004)

Inside the Yokohama International Port Terminal

Entrance to the Yokohama International Port Terminal

with that political moment I considered the issue of iconography, and more generally the issue of representation.

That realization again triggered my interest in the idea that a building represents a set of values, a place, a community or another form of identity. That is, of course, the default condition of the architectural practice. You always have to represent certain contents. At the same time, as an architect you have to design enclosures, objects that protect a certain space from the wind, rain, sun, et cetera. At the end, you are stuck between on the one hand solving the technical problems of the architecture and on the other hand designing something that is charged with representing the world. Not presenting, but representing. And so that is where the "form with the double agenda" comes in.'

That sounds a lot like how architects in the nineteenth century approached representation. Architects back then, in the façades they designed, tried to represent not only the function of the building but also tried, as honestly as possible, to represent the organization of the building and the way its load-bearing structure worked. Did you ever study that?

'No, not really. I have read some texts on representation. Probably the most important one was Colin Rowe's essay on "Character and Composition" in his book *The Mathematics of the Ideal Villa*. Maybe you can recommend some authors?'

Not much has been written on representation in architecture recently. That is what led me to do this series of interviews. Let's continue with the 'form with a double agenda' strategy. Besides the Yokohama International Port Terminal, which of your other projects can illustrate how this strategy works?

'All projects have an element of the "form with a double agenda" in them. Even the social housing I did in Madrid. The façade of the building consists of bamboo screens that the inhabitants can operate them-selves. The result is that the image of the building changes all the time. But that is only one way of reading the building. As an enclosure, the bamboo screens protect the apartments from the sun and provide a buffer zone between inside and outside. That is the other part of the double agenda on this project.'

In that project you don't apply iconography. The 'form with a double agenda' strategy is not tied to iconographic projects as such, but can it be used in every project you do?

'Perhaps it is not an iconographic project in the sense that it relates to icons. The façade does provide a certain representation though. In typical housing, any differentiation in the façade is a deliberate differentiation in material or color. Here, however, the differentiation is generated by the inhabitants themselves. By opening or closing the bamboo screens they represent themselves.'

In his essay *The Hokusai Wave*, Zaero-Polo wrote the following:

'The strategy became the foundation of a series of commissions for local authorities, most of them in Spain . . . . Iconographies did not precede the material investigation but rather emerged as viable figures from our immersion in each project's analysis. We would collect general material about local customs and iconographies and keep that information on the table while we did site analysis and programmatic diagrams. We knew that a project was structured when a formal correlation started resonating between them.

The Villajoyosa Police Station pentagonal plan was automatically derived from the site's geometry and turned into Villajoyosa's Pentagon – a reference for the municipal police headquarters with great popular appeal – and the lattices that fortify its window were built as if they resulted from a film noir, machine gun shoot-out.

The Torrevieja Theater was modelled on the local sandstone quarries and boasts a white and faceted acoustic finish modeled like a salt crystal. Sandstone quarries and salt lakes were the basis of the local economy before tourism brought its radical transformations of the local landscape, so we were bringing back a lost arcadia.

La Rioja Centre for Technology Transfer in Logroño became a building that dissolved into a vineyard: a transparent volume covered with wires and wine leaves.

The Canarian Government Multiples III proposal in Santa Cruz de Tenerife grew into a palm-tree trunk by applying triangular *brise-soleils*, shifting gradually to maximize their sun-shading effect to a high-rise tower with a triangulated exoskeleton.'

Could you explain the design you made for the Olympic Stadium in London? How did you develop the muscle iconography that you proposed for that project?

'We were asked by the organizing committee of the Olympic Games in London to design a "look and feel" for the main area where the games would be held. We thought about how to represent this area and what message the architecture should broadcast. We quickly realized that in order to efficiently communicate what it was all about, in this case we had to produce a powerful image. We wanted to design something that was immediately understandable and digestible by the public.

I think that there are many situations in which you don't have to address representation in architecture, but that there are also certain projects in which it is very difficult to escape from it. To be effective at these projects, you have to be prepared to forget, or forgo, your moral principles (laughs).

To represent the games, we looked into flowers, English gardens, et cetera. We sprinkled these themes over the site. After a couple of failed attempts, we came up with the muscle.'

Carabanchel Social Housing in Madrid by Foreign Office Architects (2007)

Municipal Police Headquarters in La Villajoyosa, Spain, by Foreign Office Architects (2004)

The Canary Government Multiples III, Spain, by Foreign Office Architects (2005)

Municipal Theatre and Auditorium in Torrevieja, Spain, by Foreign Office Architects (2006)

La Rioja Technology Transfer Centre in Logroño, Spain, by Foreign Office Architects (2007)

Did you test the muscle iconography with an audience? Have you ever tested how a proposed iconography is read by the public?

'No, I have never done that. That could be an interesting experiment.'

You presented the muscle iconography to the organizing committee of the Olympic Games. How was it received?

'It was a success. Everybody thought it was a great idea. What we said was that they needed an idea that could be consumed in a newspaper title. There could be titles like "Muscle proposed for the Olympics" or "London's first muscle presented". The idea was flexible enough to represent the project in different contexts. So we stuck with it.

We made the design for the Olympic Games in a team. Part of that team was Populous (formerly known as HOK Sports), who eventually got the commission to design the Olympic Stadium that has now been built.

There are a number of possible relations between the form of the building, the iconography, and other aspects of the architecture, such as structure, drainage, enclosure and transparency. The dialogue

London 2012 Olympic Stadium by Foreign Office Architects (2002)

London 2012 Olympic Park by Foreign Office Architects (2002)

between the iconography and those aspects can make the representation more interesting. This battle between iconography on one side and structure on the other side can be very productive and can yield interesting technological solutions. It can, for instance, result in a specific pattern for the façade. This dialogue can weaken the iconography and let it become more multifaceted.'

Are you afraid that the iconography you are designing is too literal?

'Yes.

I don't have an adversity to iconography. In some projects it works, in other it doesn't. It depends on the client and the commission.'

Does the choice of whether or not you turn to iconography relate to how public a building is?

'It is absolutely true that when a building is more public, there is more pressure to come up with a metaphor.'

Most architects seem to base the iconography they design on the function of the building. Do you do that too? Or do you also look at the context?

'The program most of the time is irrelevant. Iconography can therefore better be related to the location, the surrounding landscape, the local culture, et cetera.

London 2012 Olympic Stadium by Foreign Office Architects

In my view, an iconography – even more so than architecture itself – should always represent a virtue. Have you ever proposed an iconography that the client or public understood as the opposite of that?

'I recently had such an experience with the design of the Ravensbourne college in London. For the envelope we proposed a composition of round windows and a pattern. In the original design, the pattern was like wallpaper and had a floral motif. We explained to the client that the offspring of this was the Arts & Crafts movement. The client objected to this idea and said that the college was an advanced institute and that this design forced them to go backwards.

In the end, the design could stay pretty much the same, although we explained it differently. The proposed iconography was just one side of the double agenda in the project. The other side was that we wanted to design a volume that would be ambiguous in terms of its scale. To achieve that, we chose that pattern. But it could be a different pattern too.

We never start a design from an image. That doesn't happen with us. We would end up with a flat metaphor. The project would lose its meaning. A building should remain slightly mysterious and ambiguous in the representation of its contents.'

But if the applied iconography is too abstract, it doesn't work either.

'If the metaphor is too abstract, it indeed doesn't work either. Then the metaphor fades away and loses its capacity to broadcast any meaning. It's a fine limit.

An interesting case here is the Guggenheim Museum in Bilbao. The project emerged at a very specific political moment. In the Basque country the industry had largely moved away. On top of that came the aim for independence from Spain. It was a sort of double hit. The problems lasted for years.

In the transformation of Bilbao, all these problems were ignored. For the Guggenheim Museum they chose an architect from Los Angeles. And Frank Gehry did his job. Whether a direct iconography is appropriate or not depends on the situation, politics and culture. Sometimes the lack of a direct reading is interesting too.'

The audio guide of the Guggenheim Museum in Bilbao tells visitors that Frank Gehry, in his design, applied the metaphor of a fish.

'I know Gehry loves fish, but I didn't know that he applied the fish iconography here. That could be true. That is interesting.'

I don't think many architects are aware of the iconographic side of that building. All the attention went to the so-called Bilbao Effect it produced.

'That influenced everybody practicing today. The upside of the Bilbao Effect is that it convinced clients and the public that investing in architecture pays off. Before that nobody was convinced of that. In that sense it's an important building. But the Bilbao Effect has its downsides too.'

Ravensbourne in London by Foreign Office Architects (2010)

Preliminary design of the Ravensbourne

Guggenheim Museum in Bilbao by Gehry Partners (1993-1997)

Could it be that part of the success of the Guggenheim Museum in Bilbao lies in the fact that Gehry applied an iconography, even if nobody knew that? That the iconography informed the form of the building in such way that something extraordinary could emerge, and that this iconography in fact was the reason the building could open up architecture and make it appeal to a larger audience?

'I don't know about that. This particular iconography or narrative of the fish doesn't relate to any of the specific conditions of the local culture. It's totally incongruous.'

What I see with a lot of architects is that in their presentation they say one thing, but then pursue a different agenda in the built reality. Do you recognize this potential tension between the presented design and the actual design, between the marketing and the reality?

'There is a tension. That is an important issue. In order to win a competition or acquire a commission you are sometimes forced to forgo a metaphor to convince a client.

This was, for instance, the case with the Yokohama International Port Terminal and the metaphor of the Hokusai Wave, although it is not so obvious. In the design process, we had not used the iconography. It was latent. But it surfaced in the presentation. And then later on, a tension emerged. The wave in the competition design was smooth, just like the organization. But during the process, that smooth form became angular. The client thought of it as a betrayal. They didn't understand that a design, under the influence of technical issues, develops in a certain way. The client was fixated on the original design and expected from us a faithfulness to the original image.

World Trade Center Memorial and Towers in New York by United Architects (2002)

In our proposal for the Olympic Games in London the opposite occurred. We thought a lot about how the public would perceive the project. We were part of a bigger team and to everything we proposed to communicate, the rest of the team responded that it was too risky. We got constant criticism. As a result, the images the rendering company made were . . . so nothing. The press therefore kept asking, "What will it be like?"

I call this "happy people Photoshopping". It is a strategy to avoid anything potentially political and anything that could cause conflict. When we eventually revealed the design, the tricky thing was how to inform the public about it.'

Because if you can't realize the design later on in the process, it might turn its back on you. Like with the Yokohama International Port Terminal. On the one hand you have to present a design and get the client and public interested, but on the other hand you have to keep enough freedom to be able to develop the design further.

You designed the Yokohama International Port Terminal in 1995. How has your thinking about iconography developed through the years? Do you continue to apply it in your designs?

'In the end, my personal interest lies more with the technical, environmental and structural performance of buildings. But I don't regret to have done iconographic architecture.

A couple of years ago I read about the distinction that the nineteenth century philosopher Charles Pierce made between icons, symbols and indices. An icon literally relates to its content. With a symbol the meaning is contingent to the content. And an index is a material trace from the content – there is no literal relation with the content.

I am very interested in the relation between the diagram and the icon. The diagram is related to the performance of the building, whereas the icon is related to its form. That relation between the diagram and the icon is something I would like to introduce into the architecture discipline. It's an approach that is very different from the one that produces symbolic architecture. In symbolic architecture the architecture is highly subservient to an external metaphor.'

Can you imagine applying iconography again in future projects?

'The architecture practice is like a war. You do anything that is necessary. But as I said, at the moment, I am personally not very interested in it.'

Who would you suggest for me to interview next?

'You should talk to Ben van Berkel. I know him to be very interested in iconography and what it can do. Within the United Architects collective, I worked with Ben van Berkel, among others, on the "United We Stand" proposal for the World Trade Center site in New York.'

Competition design of the Yokohama International Port Terminal

Interview
Ben van Berkel

'I always try to mix various architectural ingredients'

Mercedes-Benz Museum in Stuttgart, Germany, by UNStudio (2001-2006)

Ben van Berkel (1957) is a Dutch architect. Together with his wife Caroline Bos, he leads the architectural firm UNStudio with offices in Amsterdam and Shanghai. Van Berkel gives lectures around the world and is head of the postgraduate training program Städelschule Architecture Class in Frankfurt.

It is not easy to arrange an interview with the extremely busy architect. After two last-minute cancellations, it turns out during the third appointment that he does not have enough time to finish the interview, so a fourth appointment is needed.

At the beginning of the twenty-first century, various architectural firms collaborated under the name United Architects to participate in the competition to rebuild the destroyed World Trade Center in New York. Ben van Berkel and Alejandro Zaero-Polo both took part in this collaboration with their firms. The final proposal, to which both Van Berkel and Zaero-Polo had made a significant contribution, was given the title 'United We Stand' and consisted of a series of interconnected skyscrapers. The interconnections would make the skyscrapers more stable, and would provide additional escape routes in case of. The image of the skyscrapers standing together referred to a line of people who are supporting one another. Which explains the title. Unfortunately, United Architects did not win the competition. Afterwards, Van Berkel stated that the design probably put too little emphasis on the emotion of grief and the process of grieving. The design focused too strongly on the future.

After losing this competition, the various firms in the United Architects collaboration participated in a few additional competitions. One noteworthy design was that for the new building that would accommodate the European Central Bank in Frankfurt. Searching for a compact building shape that would facilitate efficient internal communication, but would still let in sufficient daylight, and that would create an entirely new and significant image, the design team ultimately chose the image of a revolving coin. This image was developed into a building defined by interlocking circular slabs. A very radical proposal. Too radical for the jury.

When I asked Alejandro Zaero-Polo, at the end of the interview with him, who I should interview next about the use of ornament, and the application of iconography within that theme, he suggested to talk with you. Why do you think that Zaero-Polo recommended you? What role does ornament play in your work?

'In history there is applied ornament and essential ornament. I have never been very interested in applied ornament. An office like Herzog & De Meuron, for example, is interested in this aspect. They work together with artists to depict the function, the theme or the location of the building in a specific way. However, it always remains an addition to the building: decoration.

The route that I have chosen is a more complex one. I've always been interested in ornament as articulation in a more linguistic context. What can you say with a building? What can the building say itself? I think

Observation deck of the World Trade Center Memorial and Towers

World Trade Center Memorial and Towers within Manhattan Skyline

World Trade Center Memorial and Towers in New York by United Architects (2002)

European Central Bank in Frankfurt am Main, Germany, by United Architects (2003)

that Alejandro Zaero-Polo identifies this approach with me and therefore recommended me.

In general, I don't think it is good if architecture is given a one-dimensional reading. You have to be able to discover it. That is why I'm so interested in cinema, literature and music. Interesting work must be listened to, viewed or read repeatedly to discover the second layer of signification.

In this context, I refer to "after images": images that linger, that you want to return to, that you want to experience again. Even after experiencing such images repeatedly, you still haven't discovered all their layers and you can't even identify all the layers. This is what I want to achieve in most of the buildings that we make.

I want to reanimate the holistic in architecture. For example, I want to think beyond the collage, I want to look beyond the separate elements such as columns and walls. The organization of a building, the programmatic allocation, the structural system . . . I want to hybridize these aspects to create a new whole. And the meaning of the building can also be part of this hybrid.

In Seoul, for example, we designed the second Galleria shopping mall as a museum. Our story is that the products in the mall are also works of art and must therefore be illuminated more brightly. Due to the light color of the floor, light is reflected back onto the products. At the same time, as a mall visitor you walk over a kind of catwalk, so that you yourself also become a work of art. Hybridization and layeredness are important themes in my work.'

What do you mean exactly with articulation? I define ornament as an explanation of the construction, organization, function, social status, and/or context of the building. In current practice, ornament is used mostly to clarify the function of the building. Is this how you use ornament?

'No, I try to find a collective articulation for various ideas. I always try to mix various architectural ingredients.

Interior of the Galleria Centercity

Galleria Centercity in Cheonan, South Korea, by UNStudio (2008-2010)

The Galleria shopping mall I mentioned has an atrium. I will explain it in layers. That atrium in itself has a diversity in scale. As a result, when you first enter the building you think that it has four or five levels. This is due to the larger balconies. As you go further into the building, it appears to have perhaps 20 levels. And when you then walk into the atrium, you see that the building only has 12 levels. The atrium provides all kinds of optical illusions, not only about the organization of the building, but also about its function. At one moment it looks like a shopping mall, at another moment like a museum. The atrium is also perceived as a kind of huge chandelier: a combination of lamps in the center of the space. All these layers come together. And together this provides the articulation of the space. The illusions are so diverse. They slide over each other, move away from each other, move towards each other. It is difficult to perceive exactly what it is all about. Everything has a double meaning.'

The articulation you are seeking is not, by definition, an explanation, but can also elicit an illusion or introduce layeredness?

'Yes, but not vagueness. It is a new explanation that is based on the idea that a segmented explanation does not exist. When you emphasize only the construction or the function of a building, that is not an explanation. In that case, other aspects of the building are repressed.'

Manimal model

In one way, by means of hybridization you merge layers together. But in another, by using layeredness, you want to enable the public to read the various layers in a specific way. This reminds me of the image you published in your book Move: the Manimal.

'The Manimal is the key. In that image, it is important that the three themes – the human, the snake and the lion – are truly intertwined with one another. There are no seams. You cannot identify a single part that has only one of the three themes.'

Does hybridization via the Manimal provide a holistic image?

'Yes, but at the same time, I want to give the holistic a new meaning. It does not have to be an idealized holistic model. It can also be a paradoxical model: full of contradictions and a dose of ugliness. The Manimal is horribly ugly.'

Dienst Uitvoering Onderwijs (DUO) in Groningen, the Netherlands, by UNStudio (2006-2011)

Over time I have started to see the beauty in it.

'Perhaps the Manimal is indeed attractive as a futuristic human. But it is certainly not a classical beauty.'

When I visited the city of Groningen for the interview with Auke van der Woud, he told me that the office building that your firm designed there is popularly known as 'the cruise ship'.

'Most people experience that building when they drive into the city on the freeway. Seen from that perspective, it does perhaps look like a cruise ship. But I never wanted the building to look like that. I am sometimes concerned about the nicknames people give to buildings. You want a building to elicit that kind of images, you want it to have nicknames. But preferably more than one.'

Does your office test how a building is experienced by the public?

'No.'

Recently, MVRDV had problems when the double apartment tower that the office designed for a new business district in Seoul reminded many people of the attacks on the World Trade Center in New York.

'What did you think about this? Did you think it was interesting that they borrowed this image from the Twin Towers? Or did you think it was a cheap stunt? That is an interesting theoretical question.'

I thought the reference was totally exciting. But architecture, in my view, is to make our lives more pleasurable, not to offend large groups of people. Consequently, a moral limit has been exceeded.

'I think it is an interesting case. I would like to brainstorm with Winy Maas on this topic sometime. I have talked with friends about this. Some of them think it was a clever publicity stunt. Others think it was a statement made at the expense of the people who will be living there.

As an architect, you are of course not an autonomous artist. In America, MVRDV made many people very angry. In that country, the office hit entirely the wrong note.'

Personally, I don't think that MVRDV conceived the design as a statement. It is curious that no one at the office saw the similarities. But this is indeed why I argue for testing the public response to designs. That could prevent these kinds of incidents.

In my interview with Winy Maas, he explained that he often uses his work politically. He likes kicking sacred cows to help architecture make progress. But I wonder whether architecture has really made any progress as a result of this MVRDV design?

'Within the oeuvre of MVRDV, it is an interesting project. In that sense, I can accept it. The problem that remains is that a one-liner is effective only briefly. And the stronger the one-liner, the shorter its effect. You have to be cautious with this approach. Architecture is not comparable with art that hangs in a museum. This art can also offend people, but then they can simply walk past it. You don't have to live in it or work in it. This is why I seek architecture that has deeper layers of experience, that is more than a single message.'

According to Michiel Riedijk, public buildings deserve more pronounced ornamentation. Winy Maas believes that museums in particular require a distinct approach. How do you see these issues?

'Personally, I am very interested in how something is consumed. Are public buildings consumed more than a house or a chair? Perhaps they are. At locations where larger masses of people are gathering, the layeredness in the architecture must go deeper to ensure that all these people want to return. Many of our projects have these deeper layers. Images from outside architecture then become a source of inspiration or a diagram that is incorporated in the design. It is all about how you translate, transform, and instrumentalize this image or diagram in such a way that the architecture remains innovative and surprising. That is very important.

I can remember the first time I saw an iPhone. I thought it was a radio. It was an entirely new combination of elements that collectively formed an object with a certain autonomy. To me, this has great attraction. Not everything has a history or must have a history.

I should point out that we, of course, find references. Previously that was the diagram – the drawing line – and I have indeed become more open about this. I've expanded the diagram into the design model, because I noticed that we used some models serially. We use the Manimal and the blob-to-box design model more frequently.

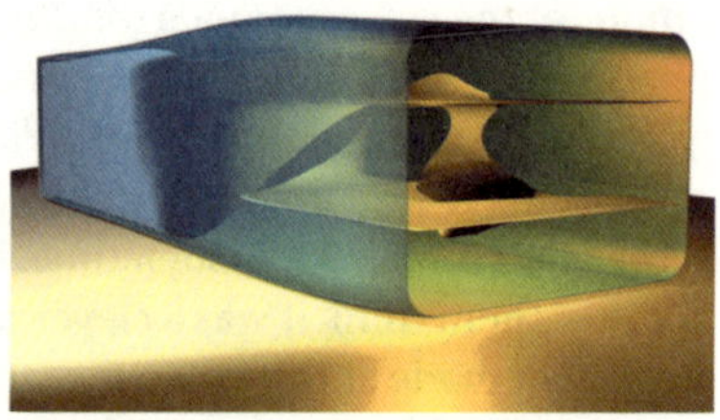

Blob-to-box model

The twist in the blob-to-box design model creates a public moment. That happens on a somewhat larger scale in the music theater that we designed in Graz and on a somewhat smaller scale in the Villa NM – which was destroyed by fire. In the center of the house, near the stairway, you could see and encounter each other. A house can also have a semi-public quality. And that twist is actually an image in itself.'

In your work you hybridize all kinds of themes. For example, the yellow-orange façade of the Agora Theater in Lelystad refers to the spectacular sunsets enjoyed by the city due to its location at the IJsselmeer and at the same time provides a colorful impulse for the rather gray city. How do you find such themes?

'You might not believe it, but I still draw a great deal. Everyone thinks that I am totally fascinated by computer technology. And I am. But I've always seen the computer as an instrument. However, it is an instrument that must be continuously developed. Similar to Andy Warhol, who discovered that you could do more with silk-screen printing technology than just make a painting: you can also use it to make decoration.

I'm confronted with many things through drawing and in that

Interior of the Mumuth Theatre

Mumuth Theatre in Graz, Austria, by UNStudio (1998-2008)

Interior of Villa NM

Villa NM near New York by UNStudio (2000-2007)

Entrance to the Agora Theatre

Interior of the Agora Theatre

Agora Theatre in Lelystad, the Netherlands, by UNStudio (2002-2007)

Interior of the Mercedes-Benz Museum

Mercedes-Benz Museum in Stuttgart, Germany, by UNStudio (2001-2006)

process I am thinking about more than the shape alone. I'm also interested in ideas. A museum like a shopping mall, for example. We presented that idea to a Chinese client.

Ultimately it all comes back to my belief that as an architect, you produce culture – whatever that is. It does not always have to be high culture. You can also flirt with the hard, plastic sides of low culture. Shopping malls for example. In Asia, shopping malls are where people meet each other, where new friendships are made. As a result, shopping malls are among the most fascinating locations possible. Face-to-face contact is still crucial. Facebook would never have happened if the founders hadn't met one another. As an architect, you must embrace such projects.

For these projects I attempt to make designs that do not tell a story as such, but that have an activating effect. Buildings must become devices.'

Can you talk about your office's design for the Mercedes-Benz Museum in Stuttgart? In the façade it seems elements are included that are derived from car design: rounded shapes, continuous windows, metallic surfaces. And in the floor plan, many people see the Mercedes star.

'I know that people like to see the star in the floor plan, and perhaps that logo subconsciously played a role as well, but the discussion in our office focused on something entirely different. We had the idea of making two exhibition spaces across from one another that would each cover a different era. When we then came up with the idea of making a double spiral of this design, we discovered that we couldn't accomplish our goals with two elements, but we needed three.

The client played an important role in this discussion. Mercedes-Benz wanted to go beyond the idea of an auto show and was looking for a spatial model that could appeal to a wider audience. With the client I discussed the helicopter that hangs in the MoMA. That is also an industrial product. If a helicopter can be art, then why can't an automobile be art as well?

I was very inspired at that time by the Rosalind Krauss book on the history of sculpture. We used various ideas from that book in the Mercedes-Benz Museum. You enter from above, walk across a landscape, walk towards something, zoom in – zoom out, everything is there.'

What fascinates me in the museum are the diagonal vistas through the atrium and the fact that you do not move from one space to another, but you can always see where you are coming from and where you are going. Ultimately, would you say this is an enormously layered concept?

'Yes. But the main concept is the idea of the Time Machine: as a visitor you drive through the museum, while the cars stand still. Time follows you, so to speak. You can no longer refer to the spatiality as Modernistic, in the sense that "I am the camera, and time and space are here before me." No, space and time are also following you.

The most interesting aspect of the Mercedes-Benz Museum is that it plays with the current era. It is as if we are living from a larger time, to a smaller time, to an even smaller time. We live simultaneously in many scales of time. That is what the museum is about.'

Did you ever present a design to a client with an active story, which you thought represented a virtue, but the client experienced the story otherwise?

(long silence) 'On occasion that has happened to me. But I always have a dialogue with the client. It is a kind of dance.

For the interior structure of the Mercedes-Benz Museum, I had always proposed concrete. The client was shocked by this. Mercedes-Benz did not stand for concrete, they said. We subsequently proposed testing the idea by placing an automobile in a concrete interior. As part of this proposal I told the story about how the concrete represents the infrastructure used by the automobile: roads, tunnels, viaducts. Concrete is a logical background for automobiles. And it also fits with the idea that you as a visitor "drive" through the building, while the actual automobiles keep standing still.'

Has the Guggenheim Museum in Bilbao – designed by Frank Gehry – been important for you? Did it change your experience of architecture or your approach to clients?

'It has been an important design. With the Guggenheim Museum it became clear that you could give architecture a particular expression, and that you could go further in that expression than I had thought until then. I therefore think it is a very refreshing building.

At the same time, however, I am also critical of it. The design led me to doubt computer architecture for the first time, because falsifications took place too. In contrast to what was happening outside, the interior consisted simply of boxes.'

In your story, you emphasize the holistic aspect of the designs and does the incorporation of images from outside of architecture play a supporting role. It is true that in your designs the iconography sometimes is so much hidden that most people will probably never consciously recognize it as one of the layers in the design.

What then fascinates me is that in your communication to the public, you do highlight this very implicit iconography. For example,

on your website one can read that your office designed a museum in China whose shape refers to ancient Chinese pots. But the iconography is so abstract that few people would consciously recognize this as a layer. Why do you write this down?

'We have always been very open about the way in which our work is created. I see that as one of the most important facets of architecture: to show how you work. By communicating about the iconography we use, we are also showing how our designs can be viewed from a cultural, even social perspective.

On that point, I believe that I view my work differently than my colleagues. I'm not particularly interested in the political-social argument. I am much more interested in how the work is created and why, and how it differs from our previous work.'

For example, you write that the shape of a museum that your office designed in Dubai refers to a type of boat in the past was used a lot in the region.

'In some cases, it is possible that I have been misleading. I also like to be someone who explains what it actually doesn't signify. Sometimes people find out about this only afterwards.' (laughs)

So we shouldn't take all references equally serious?

'No, you shouldn't.'

The National Art Museum in Beijing by UNStudio (2010)

The Museum of Middle Eastern Modern Art in Dubai by UNStudio (2008)

Collage Islands

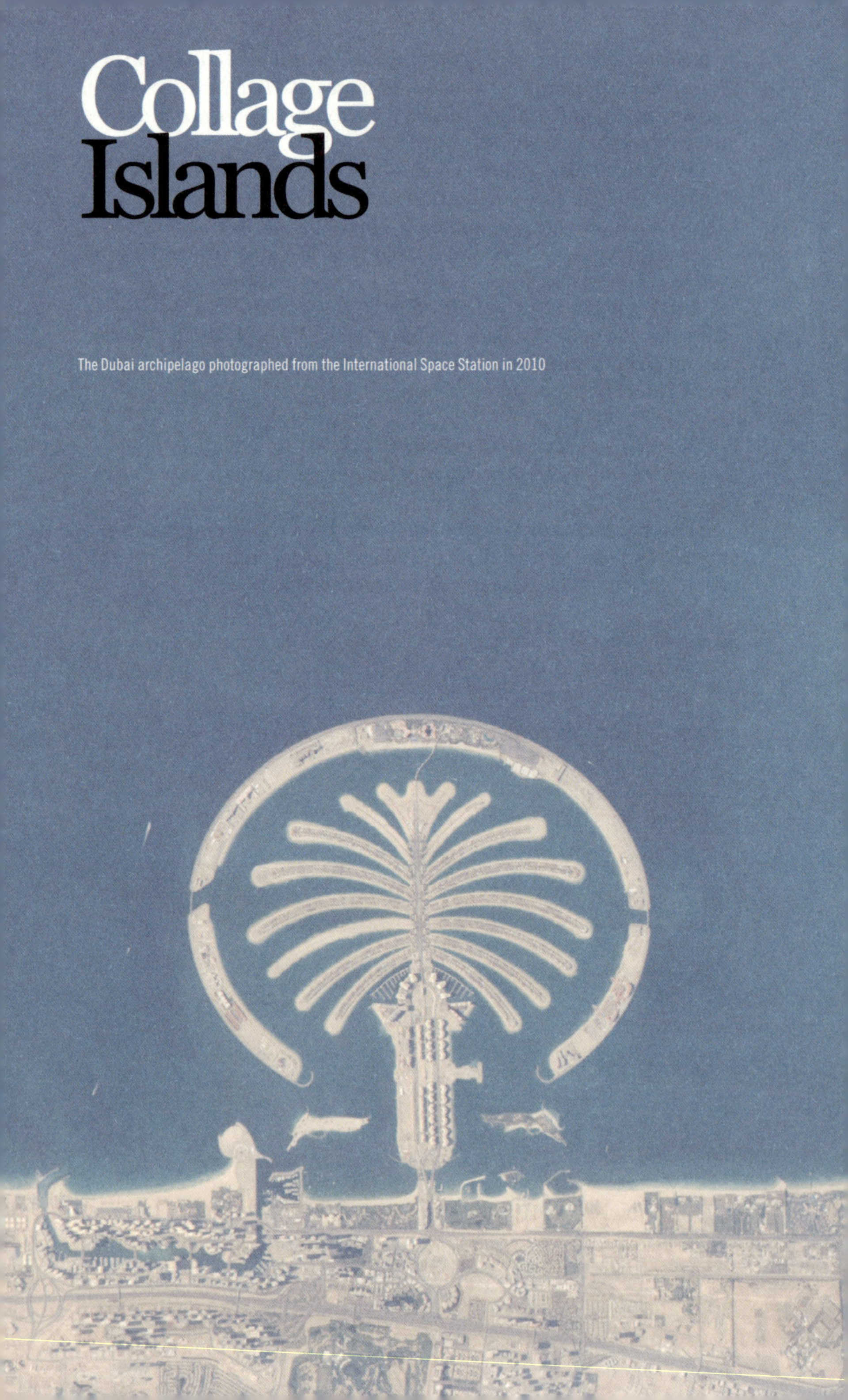

The Dubai archipelago photographed from the International Space Station in 2010

It is unknown how the idea first came about to give the peninsula this particular shape and to call it a "palm". The original design is attributed to the former emir of Dubai, Sheik Maktoum bin Rashid Al Maktoum, and was intended to boost tourism to the city – building the peninsula resulted in many additional kilometers of beach. But the young city's need for a distinctive landmark undoubtedly played a role as well.

What is known is that the idea to create a peninsula came about after the realization of a small island off the coast of Dubai on which the only seven-star hotel in the world was built: the Burj Al Arab. In the first sketches for a larger peninsula, the emir must have recognized the image of a palm. It is a clever iconography that leaves no doubt about the purpose of the peninsula: to enjoy a holiday.

In the meantime, the first Palm Island, Palm Jumeirah, is virtually complete and work is proceeding on two larger variations on the same theme, Palm Jebel Ali and Palm Deira. Further into the sea from the Palm Islands a man-made archipelago has been constructed that has been shaped like a map of the world, and there are plans for an even bigger group of islands that will depict the universe. There is certainly no lack of plans. But the required financing is another story. The credit crunch, which plunged America and Europe into a recession after 2007, has also impacted the economy of Dubai and has considerably delayed the realization of all the plans.

The construction of the Palm Islands in Dubai inspired architects and developers to propose similar plans for other locations. For the 2014 Winter Olympics in Russia, Erick van Egeraat designed an island group in the Black Sea in the shape of the Russian Federation. To emphasize the ecological dimension of his design for the Toronto Waterfront, Adriaan

Palm Jumeirah in Dubai by Nakheel (from 2001 onwards)

Architect, *Asterisk*, France, 2011

Federation Island in Sochi, Russia, by (designed by) Erick van Egcraat

Palm Jebel Ali in Dubai by Nakheel (from 2002 onwards)

The poem that circles Palm Jebel Ali says:
Take wisdom only from the wise,
Not everyone who rides a horse is a jockey.
It takes a man of vision to write on water,
Great men rise to great challenges.

Tulip Island for the coast of the Netherlands by Innovatieforum (2007)

Cedar Island for the coast of Lebanon by Noor (2009)

Geuze of West 8 designed a floating island in Lake Ontario in the shape of a maple leaf. A research group of the Dutch government has proposed the creation of new land in the North Sea in the shape of a tulip. In Lebanon, a developer proposed building an enormous island in the Mediterranean Sea in the form of a cedar tree, the national symbol of the country.

As in Dubai, these plans use the shape of a country on a map or are based on symbolic motifs. Both the maple leaf island and the tulip island were never intended to be realized as such. The plan for the maple leaf island was part of a presentation of an architectural vision, while the tulip island was primarily intended to initiate a debate about the North Sea coast of the Netherlands. However, the Federation Island and Cedar Island were intended to be realized, but turned out to be financially untenable.

Since the invention of the airplane, and later of the satellite, it has been possible to view the Earth from above and to base designs on this perspective. The possibilities offered by this new perspective were initially explored in Land Art. An influential

Toronto Waterfront by West 8 (from 2006 onwards)

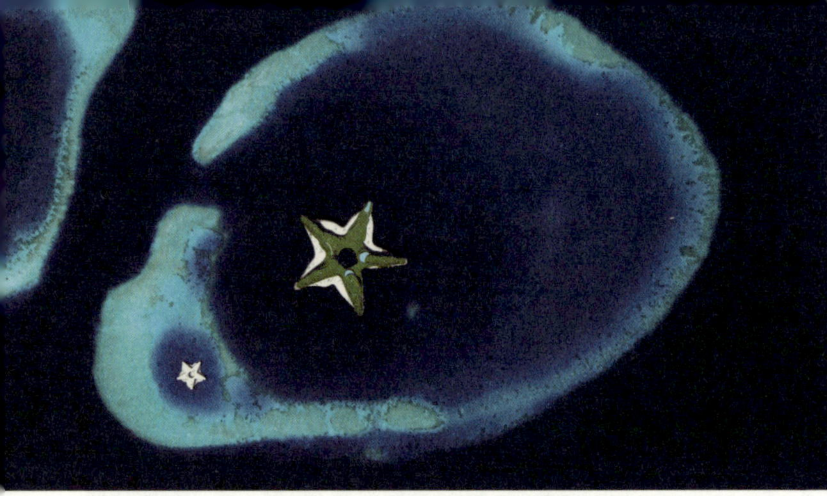

Hotel and Conference Center in the Maldives by Waterstudio.NL (from 2012 onwards)

Water Play Island in the Maarsseveense Plassen near Utrecht, the Netherlands, by Mariske Pemmelaar-Groot (2004-2005)

Superharbour between Denmark and Germany by BIG and JDS (2003)

example of this approach is the *Spiral Jetty* by Robert Smithson, which can best be viewed from the air.

In his piece, Smithson exploited the contrast between water and land. Using this contrast, he was able to create an unusually sharp image. The image is strengthened even further because the water provides a neutral background for the piece. Nothing draws attention away from the work of art.

These are factors that make designing iconographic islands so popular. The possibilities are endless. In a critical statement, the Critical Architecture Network recently designed an island in the form of a QR code. From the air, the island could be scanned with a smart phone. On the Maldive Islands Waterstudio. NL has designed a floating hotel in the shape of a starfish. Because of the limited manufacturing infrastructure on the Maldives, each leg of the "starfish" can be disconnected and then shipped elsewhere for maintenance. Off the coast of Denmark BIG has designed an artificial island in the form of a star on which all harbors of the country could be combined. In the Netherlands, in the Maarsseveense Plassen, landscape architect Mariske Pemmelaar designed a small recreational island for children in the shape of a puzzle piece. It is unclear whether children actually experience the shape of the island. From the air, however, it is spectacular image. What's more, it is an image that outstandingly portrays the function of the island.

Interview Steven Holl

'I charge an idea that drives the design'

Herning Museum of Contemporary Art in Herning, Denmark, by Steven Holl Architects (2005-2009)

Steven Holl (1947) is an American architect and principal of Steven Holl Architects in New York. Besides his work as architect, Holl is known for his writing on phenomenology in architecture. In 2012, he was awarded the AIA Gold Medal. Having no time for small talk before the interview, Holl immediately gets to the point.

How do you describe your approach to architectural design? Your designs are driven by metaphors. Is that how you talk about it?

'My work is quite complicated in the sense that I charge an idea that drives the design. I use that idea as a heuristic, self-learning device. This device gets me into to the project, steers the organization of it. And the metaphor is an idea. It is a thing within a thing, like a set of Russian dolls. But then the real measure for the architecture is not the idea. That is the experience of walking through the space: the light, the color, et cetera.

It is comparable to the work of the Russian composer Igor Stravinsky. In his compositions he occasionally used metaphors. For instance at

Idea for A Stone Box with Seven Bottles of Light driving the design of the Chapel of St. Ignatius

Interior of the Chapel of St. Ignatius in Seattle, USA, by Steven Holl Architects (1994-1997)

the beginning of a piece. But you don't have to know that to be able to appreciate the music.'

Do you use these metaphors, or ideas as you call them, also as communication devices? Do they help you to explain your designs to your clients and to a wider audience?

'Absolutely. It's also a way to communicate the project.

Some years ago I was asked to design a chapel for the Seattle University campus. At the presentation of the design there were these quirky people from the university, the president, and the people from the campus administration. A diverse and difficult audience to talk to. The metaphor I used for the design was "a stone box with seven bottles of light". This metaphor organized the design in a way that each of these "bottles of light" corresponded to one of the spiritual exercises. With this metaphor everybody immediately understood what the design was about.'

Did the metaphor in this case also represent anything?

'No. The metaphor was about the conditions of light that would be brought in. There are seven roof lights, certainly not seven bottles. The project is about elements that have a distinct quality and are simultaneously part of a whole. It is also about complementary colors.

When applying metaphors to architectural design I think it is very important not to be too literal. One of the problems in architecture and art today is that it's overly literal. One of the great things about poetry, for instance, is that in its arrangement a lot is left unknown. Architecture stays around for a long time and therefore needs many layers of meaning. The iconic building in that sense might well be the opposite of a great piece of architecture.

Daeyang Gallery and House in Seoul by Steven Holl Architects (2008-2012)

In my view architecture is at its best when, after entering, you are immersed in it. Not when you look at it from the outside. For me the experience is the most important.

But can you use a metaphor? Yes. I think one of the great things about the death of Deconstructivism, the death of Postmodernism, the death of everything, is that architecture has become completely open. That makes it really exciting to be an architect right now.

In South Korea I am doing a project that is based on a piece of music that was written in 1976 by a Hungarian-Canadian composer. It is a piece that has never been played, because the required orchestra was too large. They've never been able to fund a performance. And now I have taken this piece of music and have interpreted it as a piece of architecture. It is an incredible project. After the collapse of the "–isms" everything opened up. There is no longer a true way to do architecture; there is no common language. It's up to our imagination.'

Isn't it weird to design a building in South Korea based on a music piece from a completely different context?

'I would say that you can use anything as a metaphor, but that you can't just transplant in onto a site regardless of the conditions of the site. The local climate, the culture, the environment, et cetera, should play a role in the design. As an architect you cannot just make a scribble for either one site or another. I feel very strongly that the project in some way should connect to the urban context.

I also want to say this: for an architect it is crucial to spot the conditions that can drive the design towards realization.'

The Residence at the Swiss Embassy in Washington by Steven Holl Architects (2001-2006)

Where does the idea that drives the design stem from? Is it based on the program, the client, the context . . . or can it really be just anything?

'No, it absolutely cannot be anything. The intention in architecture is enormously important. The intention of the client, but also the intention you have as architect.

Take for instance the residence that I designed for the Swiss ambassador in Washington D.C. When working on the design I thought about how a residence like this is a visual testimony of a nation's cultural standards. It's not a normal private house, but an official residence. The exterior appearance and interior design are a calling card with which Switzerland presents itself to the United States. The standards and self-image of the country are measured and judged by the building. The search for an appropriate image led to a combination of the traditional and the modern that corresponds with that of Switzerland, which lives

Idea for a Body - Battleground for Invisible Forces driving the design

Knut Hamsun Center in Hamarøy, Norway, by Steven Holl Architects (1994-2009)

Interior of the Knut Hamsun Center

in the presence of its history, yet also is dedicated to a new, progressive spirit. The materiality of the residence is an important feature of the design. The building's charcoal color concrete and sand-blasted translucent structural glass planks were inspired by the black rocks and white snow of the Swiss Alps. The functional cross layout of the house playfully points to the white cross of the Swiss national flag.

When I got the assignment to design the Knut Hamsun Center in Hamarøy in Norway, I reread a lot of the stories that Knut Hamsun had written over the years. The whole building became an interpretation of his texts. From that I could conceive the building as a "body – battleground for invisible forces". The perimeter wall here is a body that inside holds a crisscrossing route. At certain points this route cuts through the perimeter wall to form windows and balconies. Although it is a center for literature, the main problem was the light. The building is located above the Arctic Circle, so in the summer there is plenty of light while in the winter there is hardly any. In the end for me this was a very successful project, as it started out from something that was integral to it: the texts of Knut Hamsun.

A project, which is similar in that sense, is the Herning Museum of Contemporary Art in Denmark. The amount of work the museum owns of the Arte Povera movement makes it of global importance. The museum has the largest collection of work by artist Piero Manzoni, except for the Manzoni Foundation itself. The Danvo family, that started the museum, has always supported Manzoni, This family owned the former shirt factory that is located across the street from the museum. This factory building still houses part of the art collection and was designed in the form of a shirt collar. In the end everything was connected to this wonderful textile factory. So the whole project revolves around this idea of the cloth. Viewed from above the shape of the building resembles a collection of shirtsleeves, sleeves that bring light into the galleries. The white concrete walls have a cloth texture.

Once you have an idea that drives the design, you try to find the language that is appropriate to that idea. A language that is particular to the project. This idea of the cloth makes the project more meaningful to the collection, the people who visit the museum, and for the people who live around the museum.

Just as important was that this idea of the cloth turned the museum into an original project. I had never before done a project where I threw cloth in the formwork of the concrete to have the wall wrinkled. I probably won't do that again, because it makes this project what it is. The hard part of having many projects is not to repeat oneself. I want to make original projects.'

The metaphor of the sleeves and cloth in the Herning Museum of Contemporary Art is quite literally translated into architecture. When does a metaphor, or iconography, become too literal? Are you afraid to reach that point?

'When a project loses its ability to have multiple meanings, it has become too literal. That is the part where a project becomes kitschy. That is the problem we face today, but in a way it is a problem we always had. We should try to think in many, many depths.

So yes, I am afraid of making the metaphors in my projects too literal. But as an architect you don't have full control over this. A critic, for instance, can reread a project that forever changes the way you see it. In his book *The Iconic Building* architecture historian Charles Jencks, in a picture, compared the Sydney Opera House with a couple of fornicating turtles. With this literal metaphor he ruined this incredible piece of architecture for many people. In a way it's a kitschy thing to do

Herning Museum of Contemporary Art in Herning, Denmark, by Steven Holl Architects (2005-2009)

Detail of the wrinkled concrete façade of the Herning Museum of Contemporary Art

One of the galleries in the Herning Museum of Contemporary Art

for a critic. Our ability to deeply read this very complicated work of architecture is hereby flattened out.

The Sydney Opera House has these marvelous layers of space, performs amazingly in the public realm of the city, really has turned the harbor into a place . . . . This might well have been the first time that, let's say, an iconic piece of architecture has given meaning to a city and even a country. People now talk about the Bilbao effect. This was 1958. On many levels it is an incredible building.

The same thing happened to me when architecture critic Herbert Muschamp in the *New York Times* called the very complicated dormitory building that I had designed for MIT in Cambridge a kitchen sponge. It was indeed the idea of "porosity" that structured the design. The slab with rooms had a load-bearing façade that worked like an exoskeleton. Inside the slab was hollowed out to form grotto-like common rooms. The main ambition with the design was to make public spaces in the interior. Muschamp's simplistic reading cancelled out all these other layers of meaning that I had designed.'

In Knokke-Heist, Belgium, you designed a hotel above an existing casino. The shifted, planar form of the hotel suggests the sails of a boat, which is a reference to the mural in the casino below by artist René Magritte depicting a sailboat. Are these metaphors meant to be read and understood by the public?

'The idea or metaphor should first and foremost work out well in space and light. The experience that I already mentioned. I prefer it when people can't recognize the idea upfront. It should be more subtle than that. Otherwise it turns glib.'

But people that return to the building might recognize the iconography of the sail as one of the layers of the design?

'Right.

In Amsterdam I designed a pavilion for a local housing cooperative. There were two ideas that drove this design. The first idea was about the color scheme that is inscribed in the architecture. This was derived from a piece of music called "Patterns in a Chromatic Field" by the American composer Morton Feldman. The indeterminate music is echoed in the indeterminate positioning of color patches throughout the pavilion. The second idea was to make a fractal and porous architecture in which the plan and section were essentially the same. Here I referred to the Menger sponge: a fractal cube that was invented by the Austrian mathematician Karl Menger.

The program called for a space in which different types of events could take place. People had to be able to lunch there, have meetings, have parties. The pavilion also had to orientate the existing building towards the canal. So there were quite some practical requirements driving the design.

To experience and appreciate the built pavilion, you do not neces-

Simmons Hall at the campus of MIT in Cambridge, USA, by Steven Holl Architects (1999-2002)

Sail Hybrid in Knokke-Heist, Belgium, by Steven Holl Architects (2005)

sarily have to know the references to the indeterminate music or the Menger sponge. It is actually more interesting that you can't tell what it is. That I used two interlocking ideas here probably helped. Each idea cancels out the obvious reading of the other. So using two ideas instead of one is a good technique to create a layered design.'

Sydney Opera House by Jørn Utzon (1957-1973)

Interior of the Sarphatistraat Offices

Detail of the interior of the Sarphatistraat Offices

Sarphatistraat Offices in Amsterdam by Steven Holl Architects (1996-2000)

In my view, architectural metaphors, like architecture itself, should represent a virtue. Have you ever proposed a metaphor that the client didn't perceive as such?

'Not really. I have certainly proposed designs that were rejected. A rule of thumb is that the more intelligent the client is, the greater the possibility is to do an important piece of architecture. It is therefore always great to work for universities: there is always a group of intelligent people who can analyze your ideas on many levels.

That is also one of things that I found in China when working there. There was such a thirst for new ideas. Everything was possible. After the Olympic games, however, the climate has changed. It is not easy to work there anymore. It is now much more exciting to work in the United States and Colombia. In Bogotá I am working on a university building. Because the climate is quite even through the year, I had this idea to turn the building inside out and create several spaces in the open air.'

Do you feel that your architecture connects in a certain way to an architectural tradition?

'(Silence) I don't see my work as part of a tradition. On the contrary, it breaks with it. Great architecture is so great because it is about the eternal return. This is a concept of eternal beauty from an era in which time wasn't as linear as it is now.

In my architecture I try to discover the possibilities of the unknown. This, I think, is an optimistic condition. Our future depends on our ability to imagine, to think and to develop technologies that lead us to an open future. So my architecture might connect with some traditions, but at the same time aims to transcend them to build a new future.

The extension of the Nelson-Atkins Museum of Art in Kansas City was about relating to the past, in that case an old neoclassical building. One of the most powerful parts of the project is the moment that you look back from the glass "lenses" to the old building. The complex of buildings continuously opens up and throws you into this dialogue between the new and the old. It's not something you can photograph. You have to be there to experience it.

So I would say I do relate to architectural traditions, I respect the authenticity of them, but I strive to design something that is completely new.'

When did these metaphors, or ideas, start to drive your designs?

'From the very beginning. One of the first freestanding structures that I did was a beach house whose design was inspired by Herman Melville's novel *Moby Dick*. The story goes that when an Indian tribe would find a whale skeleton on the beach, they would pull it on land and stretch skins over it to transform it into a house. This practice happened not far from the location of the house. In the design this is reflected in a wooden exoskeleton that runs around the house. This was 1984.

When I had started my practice four years before, Postmodernism was being hyped. I hated it, along with Deconstructivism. So I had to find another way to make architecture. I wanted to make something that was less predictable and something in which the language was implied. That is where it began.

I have to say that I prefer the word idea over the word metaphor.'

Do the metaphors in your work connect your architecture to art?

'Sure. Art and architecture have increasingly grown integral. I worked with artist Walter de Maria at the Nelson-Atkins Museum on a space where you can't see where the architecture ends and the art starts. Both disciplines have merged. It's a piece called *One Sun 34 Moons*, which is

Doctorate's Building of the National University of Colombia in Bogotá by Steven Holl Architects (2010)

Installation One Sun 34 Moons by Walter de Maria in the parking garage of the Nelson-Atkins Museum of Modern Art

The Nelson-Atkins Museum of Art in Kansas City, USA, by Steven Holl Architects (1999-2007)

Overview of the Nelson-Atkins Museum of Art

House in Martha's Vineyard, USA, by Steven Holl Architects (1984-1988)

the centerpiece of the expansive granite-paved entrance plaza with a reflecting pool that forms a new entry space shaped by the existing building and our new addition. I deferred to Walter as I hoped his work would engulf the entrance experience. The "moons" of the artwork are circular skylight discs at the bottom of the pool that bring water-refracted light into the garage below. These were already part of our scheme, but Walter moved them around to integrate them into his piece, and added a gold "sun" disc in the middle.

The design for the façade of the Storefront for Art and Architecture was a collaboration with artist Vito Acconci. To be able to literally open up the gallery to the street we introduced a series of hinged panels made of fiber concrete. It was supposed to be a temporary work. But they have rebuilt it to make it permanent. Art, in a way, became architecture.

The connection that has been established between architecture and art forms a fertile ground for all kinds of new collaborations. In these collaborations lies part of the future of architecture.'

Storefront for Art and Architecture in New York by Steven Holl Architects (1992-1993)

Interview
Winy Maas

'The building as an advertisement is very suitable for certain functions.'

Cartoon and Animation Museum in Hangzhou, China, by MVRDV (2011–2015)

Winy Maas (1958) is a Dutch architect and urban planner. Together with Jacob van Rijs and Nathalie de Vries, he is a managing director of the architectural firm MVRDV. Their office is located in a renovated factory building in Rotterdam.

'Am I being interviewed now?', asks a surprised Winy Maas when one of his colleagues introduces me. The appointment for the interview had actually been made months in advance. 'What is the interview about?', asks Maas. When I tell him it's about the building as ornament, he responds: 'But I don't know anything about that.' The first question of the interview is therefore his and not mine.

'What is your definition of the building as ornament?'

I speak of the building as ornament when an image from outside architecture is included into an architectural design to explain the function or the context of that design. According to architecture historian Auke van der Woud, when viewed from the nineteenth-century context, ornament is essentially an explanation of the function and social status of a building.

'The definition of Auke van der Woud is useful. Ornament is something you don't need for its function, but functionally you do need it. That is comical. You use non-functional aspects to increase the effectiveness of the building.

Ornament has been a dirty word for many years. That changed due to architecture offices such as Herzog & De Meuron. The Bird's Nest Stadium that they designed in Beijing represents a culmination of that new ornamentation.'

Winy Maas almost stumbles over the word ornamentation. It seems like he is assessing the word for its usability.

'The design of the Bird's Nest Stadium immediately shows how complex this topic is. It touches on so many themes. On the one hand, the ornamentation resulted in an incredible amount of steel being required to build the stadium. It is an extremely non-ecological design. It's not purist, a Calvinist could never have imagined it. On the other hand, the image of the bird's nest elicits the feeling that the building has something to do with nature, and not with political ideology, sociology or teaching a moral lesson. In China, I think that was enormously important. That explains why the building could be built. I'm not saying whether the building is good or bad. It is an impressive design. Herzog & De Meuron used a very effective method. At this point, we should supplement Auke van der Woud's definition. Besides the function and status of a building, the social and political context in which it operates is also important.'

One of the reasons for this interview was to discuss your office's design for the Comic and Animation Museum in Hangzhou, China. How did that design come about?

'For this museum I wanted to design spaces in which you would be surrounded by the comics, as if you were actually in the comics. I wanted to create spaces without any horizon, or in any case without corners. That was the concept.

Raising the balloon-shaped volumes ensured that the neighboring Hangzhou Lake, which the local population considers to be very beautiful, was given more space. You can see the lake through the building, and even sail underneath the building. The raised balloons then had to be connected with the ground for the entrances and so forth. At that point, the design could be linked with its primary message: it is all about comics. The speech balloon – the museum is almost the spokesperson for that medium – is the iconic image that best communicates the message.'

Library within the Cartoon and Animation Museum

How was the design received in China?

'We were one of five architecture offices invited to submit a design for the museum. Compared to the other designs, our proposal was compact, which left a lot of open space around the building. That aspect appealed to the jury.'

So it was about much more than just the iconic image?

'Yes, but that image certainly helped. An additional advantage of the speech balloon is its flexibility. If it turned out during the planning process that a larger building is needed, then the speech balloons can be expanded.'

How do you position this design in your oeuvre? With this design, you are taking an entirely new direction.

'I didn't say that.'

It's what I say.

'For the record: museums are daft things. In architectural history, museums have a strange position. They are collective buildings. And museums serve their collection, but at the same time, they have to show from the outside what is happening inside, and thereby attract people.

We once made a design for the National Palace Museum located just south of Taipei, the largest city in Taiwan. This design sheds light on a different side of ornamentation, if you use that word. The collection of the museum was a stolen collection. The historical objects were collected by the Taiwanese on mainland China and brought to the island about forty years ago. It is comparable to all the stuff that the French took from Egypt and then erected at the Place de la Concorde and elsewhere. All very questionable. In any case, our initial question was, what would be the best museum for that collection? We first designed an abstract building – which in itself is just as ornamental – that took a neutral position with respect to the collection. We then raised that "Miesian box" and placed it on top of a mountain. It is like Noah's Ark, just barely touching the ground. The museum has "landed" on a high point of the island. With this gesture, the delicate moral position of the museum is amplified. This makes the museum different from other museums, and consequently also attractive. It is, as you describe it, functional in an extended sense.'

This indeed explains the function of the building.

'I think that this is best seen in the designs of museums.'

Besides the design for the Comic and Animation Museum, MVRDV recently made a design for another museum. Together with the Danish architecture office COBE, in 2011 MVRDV won the design competition for the Danish Rock Museum in Roskilde. Above old factory buildings, the two architecture offices projected three new volumes. The first volume will accommodate the rock museum. The second volume will contain student housing. And the third volume, which looks like a stack of loudspeakers, will accommodate the offices of the annual Roskilde Rock Festival. The factory buildings behind and under these new volumes will be largely left open and can be used for all kinds of events. One section of the factory buildings will be used for the Roskilde Festival Folk School.

The pointed façade panels on the museum portion of the building complex in Roskilde are strongly reminiscent of the metal studs on the armbands, shoes and jackets sometimes worn by rock music fans. Was that association intentional?

'These are actually acoustic panels that make it possible to give concerts around the building. These panels are a way to slightly temper the cacophony of sound that will occur during such events. The fact that the panels appeal to the Roskilde feeling is a bonus. For the client, that

National Palace Museum in Taipei, Taiwan, by MVRDV (2005)

Rockmagneten in Roskilde, Denmark, by MVRDV and COBE (2011)

One of the Rockmagneten's courtyards

was also a reason to spend money on such an acoustic absorption pattern. The client understands their function. It gives the building an address.'

Why do you think it is not illogical to integrate an element from outside architecture into architecture?

'It is all about the story! At a certain moment you have to judge a design on its narrative too, on what it intends to do. That is where architecture ultimately proves itself. Of course, some stories are better than others. As an architect, you have to develop a critique, and learn why some stories are better than others.'

Do you experience tension between wanting to tell a story and not wanting to make the references too literal? Do you think a certain abstraction in the ornament is important?

'I always say that you should want to keep coming back to a building. If I hear the word "abstraction", then I think about something that you don't want to see more than once. The one-liner must have sufficient depth. But you should also not shun the one-liner. So many nondescript buildings are already being built.'

In 2010, the elongated residential complex Confluence was completed in the French city of Lyon. Five architectural firms each designed one segment of this complex; MVRDV was responsible for the southernmost part. The façade of that part of the building features aluminum shutters decorated with letters. Together, the letters constitute the first article of the European Constitution.

'The fact that the apartment building expresses itself towards the city with this text, originated from agitated feelings about the French politics, as well as the Dutch politics. The fact that this bunch of morons in 2005 did not vote for the European Constitution: it doesn't make any sense! As if we're living on Mars. During the week that we were working on the design, I was really angry about this. At that point I thought: let's show this anger in the building.

By placing part of the European Constitution on the façade, the building is anchored to a specific time in history. Plenty of buildings are being realized that could just as easily have been conceived a decade ago. I prefer to design something that is truly of the moment, in this case the specific political context of that moment. The building has become a big advertisement for the European Constitution. Yes, that is fairly literal. The beauty of the design is that the sixty families that live in the building have each been given one word to care for. If they open a shutter, that word is no longer legible. These families have all become involuntary partners in the advertisement.

In films from the 1970s and 1980s, you sometimes have a character lying in a bedroom, and outside the bedroom window a neon sign

Le Monolithe in Lyon, France, by MVRDV (2004-2010)

blinks on and off all night. It's an image that I really like. As resident you are suddenly part of a larger whole. For example, you are sleeping behind the C of Coca-Cola. I think that is a good address, viewed from both inside and outside. The apartments step out of that endless neutrality and introversion that is associated with housing. I find that fascinating.'

The relationship between the individual dwelling and the neon sign you describe returns in your work in the design that MVRDV created for three apartment buildings in Hoek van Holland, which were shaped like the letters . . .

'. . . HvH.'

Alphabet Building in Amsterdam by MVRDV (from 2011 onwards)

Villa VPRO in Hilversum, the Netherlands, by MVRDV (1994-1997)

Teletech Campus in Dijon, France, by MVRDV (2010-2012)

Didden Village in Rotterdam by MVRDV (2002-2006)

For that location, at the entrance to the port of Rotterdam and on the 'corner' (hoek) *of Holland, this was a clear gesture. Recently your firm also presented a design for an office building in Amsterdam, in which the windows are shaped like the letters of the alphabet.*

'The design of course refers to a printer's type case. We designed that office building for a design agency, Thonik, which will rent the top floor. For them, the façade is an indirect advertisement.'

Did Thonik also design the font?

'Yes, they are even marketing it.

I have nothing against the word "advertisement". In this interview, I have already used it twice. The building as an advertisement, that is very suitable for certain functions. You then move in the direction of the building as an icon. You want to make something exemplary.

Of course, such a font is not flexible. It is 2011. That is the limitation of architecture. But is that such a terrible thing? I have my doubts about that. It can become boring. But on the other hand, a client also wants to see something of himself back in the architecture. This does offer room for that.'

So you are not afraid to be contemporary? In France, you updated the façade of an existing office building by adding a huge QR code to it. Didn't you go too far there?

'Of course, a feature like a QR code can quickly become outdated. But as time goes on, the client can change the message communicated by the QR code, so that it updates itself.'

Generally speaking, do you think the urban landscape is rather boring?

'Yes, I think there should be more possibilities for individualism. Difference is also an expression of freedom. I am a proponent of a more Asiatic style of urban planning.'

Has the ornamental side of your office's work become stronger over the years, or was it already present in your early work?

'The advertisement-like aspects have been present for some time. Firstly, we have always been interested in directness. Secondly, we have always focused strongly on the process and the communication of the design. We always believed that non-architects should also be able to understand a building. Then it is about the message of the building, what you want to achieve with that message. That is our interpretation of the word "icon". It is not so much about shape, but much more about expressing, as clearly as possible, the added value of the design.

Our first design, the office building for the VPRO broadcasting company in Hilversum, has a non-façade. We wanted to display the interior of the building. We first conceived of the façade as air, but of course it had to be executed in glass. You can see that it was difficult for us to make that façade. Consequently, it is probably ornamental as well.

But in this way you can see the structure of the hilly interior from the outside. From inside the building, you can also see the surroundings. We included the suggestion of endlessness in the design.

The small houses that we designed in Rotterdam on top of an existing warehouse were also strictly ornamental with their Yves Klein blue color. In this way, we could create a mini-sky in the attic and show that we were expanding the city in the vertical direction. By building on rooftops, you can keep the middle class in the city. You have to almost shout this message. I could have also done this in a Swiss-like fashion, but then no one would have seen the message. And I could have painted the apartments orange, but then the message would have been interpreted incorrectly. But with the Yves Klein blue color, the houses become heavenly, they are light and cheerful, and by now they have almost become part of the protected cityscape. So we have come rather far with that daft, 40 square meter roof structure. It is a messenger.

And that messenger has been part of our work for a long time. A classic Dutch problem is how you can avoid preaching your message. With sufficient abstraction, content and depth, nuance and perspective . . . you can avoid that preaching.'

Therefore you didn't want to decorate the blue houses with clouds or the text 'this is a good way to densify the city.'

Glass Farm in Schijndel, the Netherlands, by MVRDV (2008-2013)

'No, because in the case of the blue houses, the design is self-explanatory.

But regarding the textual explanation that you mentioned, in Schijndel we designed a farmhouse. It is a building clad in glass on which we printed a photograph of a farmhouse. We essentially took the average of the farmhouses that we encountered in the area. The way we arrived at that average, the methods that we used, is explained on the façade. At the moment I am wondering: why do we do that? That fascinates me, to also directly explain that average.'

Why did you use the image of the farmhouse there?

'It was the only volume that the village at that location would accept. During World War II, Schijndel was bombed by the Americans. On one remaining vacant lot in the village, the municipality wanted to realize a new building. A long discussion took place in the village about how big that new building should be. We visualized the various options. The various sightlines had to be maintained, this one and that one (With his hands Maas cuts pieces of an imaginary volume). At that point I said: that looks like a farmhouse. However, this farmhouse is 1.8 times bigger than the average farmhouse.'

This means you couldn't have made a replica?

'No, the building volume was too large for that. But like many other villages, Schijndel is no longer a village as such, it has become a small town. By enlarging the farmhouse proportionally, you could also express this expansion. And the building is clad in glass, because it is a ghost of a farmhouse.

Interior of the Glass Farm

When we found the technology to burn the image onto the glass, we could expand the story. In the composite photograph of the average farmhouse, which we made together with Frank van der Zanden, we could show the enlargement factors. On the photograph, you could also open a window and look inside. And you could include messages. It's a nice game.

Because it is a glass farmhouse, in the evening the building transforms into a lantern. This strengthens the message even more.

A replica would have been immediately accepted in the village. But that gets you nowhere, because then you don't take a single step forward.'

So you like to give a design a certain twist?

'Yes. We like to give things a boost.'

It can't be too easy?

'No, preferably not.'

One flood-proof houses that MVRDV designed for New Orleans, USA (2007)

School in New Orleans, USA, by MVRDV (2006-2007)

So it always has to be at least slightly different?

'Well, what legitimizes the word "different"? You discover shortcomings in a process and you want to express them.

After the flooding in New Orleans, we were asked to redesign the old houses, but adapted to contemporary requirements. This was a very clear assignment. So we did exactly what we were asked to do. Is there any reason for us to disguise this? Nevertheless, everyone was shocked by our directness. In this case, architecture suddenly became the bearer of the message. Sometimes people do not want to see the message. Then they only want to see how nice and fine everything is. Even irony, which is certainly needed following such a calamity, is too much then.

Anyway, what is controversial? I think that something controversial helps to sharpen the definition.'

But should buildings proclaim such messages?

'At our office, we think they should. We are essentially urban planners and we therefore view buildings in a wider context. Of everything that is built on earth, ninety-five percent is shit. By commenting on this situation, we want to help improve it.'

Another point: where does your current fascination for hills and mountains come from?

'I must acknowledge that we are indeed strongly fascinated with landscape. That is probably because I was trained as a landscape architect.

The question you are really asking is: when is a hill right? In our book *KM3*, we explained that the hill is one of the ways to both create density as well as sell it. Density in the sense that housing and offices are combined with public domain. With a hill, you can create a publicly accessible roof and place the program underneath.

Our design for the Serpentine Pavilion in London is an example of such a hill. In the series of pavilions, you should show for once what the construction of a pavilion actually does to Hyde Park. You build something, but at the same time you remove it from the public space. I would like an institute such as the Serpentine to be service-minded and create a hill with a publicly accessible roof. During the construction of the pavilion, the grass of Hyde Park would be briefly raised. During its dismantling, the grass would come back down. I still regret that it was never built. Due to the Health and Safety regulations, it became too expensive. It was the most curious episode in the history of the Serpentine Pavilion, which actually strengthens the design.

A second line of logic about making a hill emerged from our design for a school in New Orleans. Something had to be done with the debris left behind by Hurricane Katrina. What could be better than to make a hill by pushing all the debris together? Then you can see what happened, it becomes tangible. And why shouldn't a school nestle in that hill? This was my very simple political message. For that matter, the design had

Serpentine Gallery in London by MVRDV (2004)

Power Center in Gwanggyo, South Korea, by MVRDV (2007)

another advantage. In America, people are always talking about New Urbanism: buildings should be designed in traditional style. By locating the school in a hill, we could avoid that style discussion. The building simply becomes landscape.

In America, the design of schools however is close to the most sacred topic there is. You cannot touch that. I enjoy giving the discussion about schools a boost though.'

The building as advertisement is about representation in the vertical plane. With buildings in the form of hills, you can avoid a discussion about representation. Are these hills therefore the opposite of the building as advertisement?

'No. Our design for the Serpentine Pavilion advertised that it would have been better if the park would continue.'

So the advertisement and that hill are linked together?

'Yes. The school that we designed in New Orleans would make it possible for people to flee to a higher point if there was another flood. According to Dutch probability calculations, there is always a risk that the levees will fail once every hundred years. Consequently, the hill also advertises the following message: guys, we don't trust your levees.'

In China, your office designed a building complex in the shape of a hilly landscape. In that design the hill is not walkable, it appears to be primarily about the image.

'That design connects to the discussion about "Chineseness". In response to the design of the Bird's Nest Stadium, every foreign architect is being asked to design a Chinese building. Whatever that is. We are always asked: "How Chinese is your building?"'

Always?

'Yes, almost always. In this case, our ambition was to combine high-rise construction with terraces. Would that be possible? A building in which everyone has an outdoor space, where all the outdoor areas together – due to their consistent planting – would create a vertical park. With an integrated drainage system. To cool the building, we wanted to use the Dew Harvester, which we developed together with the Delft University of Technology. Under certain conditions it allows you to convert dew into cooling water. All those aspects were incorporated in the design.

The fact that the complex has a hilly appearance is a bonus. That makes the communication of the design simple and direct. The high-rise district has become a landscape. You indeed get an uneasy feeling in your stomach: is this kitsch or not?'

And is this Chinese or not?

'The design supports us with the polemics that are required of you in Chinese urban planning. This appeals to the Chinese enormously. It is a hit. We have been approached by several parties who also want to have the design. I think that is rather humorous, that you could build the same design on multiple locations.'

Does your firm design differently for the Chinese than for other nationalities, such as the Dutch?

'In principle, we don't. But Chinese culture is of course different. As an architect, you develop a rapport with all kinds of places in the

Mirador in Madrid by MVRDV (2001-2005)

world. This requires concentration. You study construction methods, legal aspects, society . . . . You can only hope that your architectural proposal in other countries strikes the same chord that you would have wanted in the Netherlands. You engage in the same dialogue. We are very interested in the reactions. We want to use our designs to encourage the discussion about what is meaningful and important, also at locations that you perhaps don't know that well. At these locations, you have to hypothesize. You can sometimes go wrong: in that case you haven't understood the assignment well enough, you have been too brazen, and you don't get the job. That can happen.'

Have you ever made a design for a building as ornament, in a manner of speaking, which the client thought was all wrong?

'Our design for the National Palace Museum in Taiwan is an example of that situation. Our design was not chosen. The image of that unsteady volume on top of that mountain was . . .'

Too sensitive?

'Yes. We always make something very pronounced. Sometimes it is well received, sometimes not. That is the risk of our profession.'

Are you in a way also proud that you were not selected?

'No, I would have been much prouder if our design had been selected. A design that does strike a chord, but at the same time triggers aggression and is rejected, is the second best option.'

In a new neighborhood with only perimeter blocks in the Spanish capital Madrid in 2005 MVRDV realized a freestanding slab that protruded high above its surroundings. Instead of a courtyard garden, the firm created a roof garden on the 12th floor.

'With the Mirador in Madrid, we built an apartment building at a location where that was actually not permitted. In every lecture I will say how much I respect Spanish culture, that they accepted such criticism. Ultimately, this is more beneficial to that culture.'

A little less than a month after the interview with Winy Maas, MVRDV presented their design for dual apartment towers for a new high-rise district in the South Korean capital Seoul. The design, called The Cloud, consisted of two apartment towers connected at the mid-point by means of a "pixelated cloud" with shared facilities.

Immediately after the presentation of the design, reactions appeared on various websites: the design was remarkably similar to the largest explosion during the attacks on the World Trade Center in New York. Was this the architect's intention? Some respondents suggested that an architect, being an artist, should have the freedom to make such a design. Especially with Americans the design was poorly received: it seemed like a tribute to the attacks. How could an architect possibly design something like that?

The controversy grew quickly. Within 48 hours, it had reached national media all over the world, and MVRDV felt compelled to apologize for this unintended association.

'We've had quite a lot of calls from angry Americans saying it's a disgrace', explained Jan Knikker, head of Public Relations at MVRDV. '9/11 was not the inspiration behind the design, the inspiration was an actual cloud. It was not our intention to create an image resembling the attacks nor did we see the resemblance during the design process. We sincerely apologize to anyone whose feelings we have hurt.'

The design had become a criticism, but not a criticism that the architect had intended, nor was it productive one. The provocations of MVRDV are always deliberately chosen and are focused on bringing society a step further by means of debate. In that sense, the provocations always represent a virtue. Here that wasn't the case.

Within a few days, the media storm had died down. On the MVRDV team the incident however had made a deep impression. Repeated requests to discuss the incident and its consequences in a follow-up interview have been rejected to date. It was simply too sensitive. Although an element of provocation remains part of the approach of MVRDV, several months later Knikker explained that the office had experienced enough controversy for the time being.

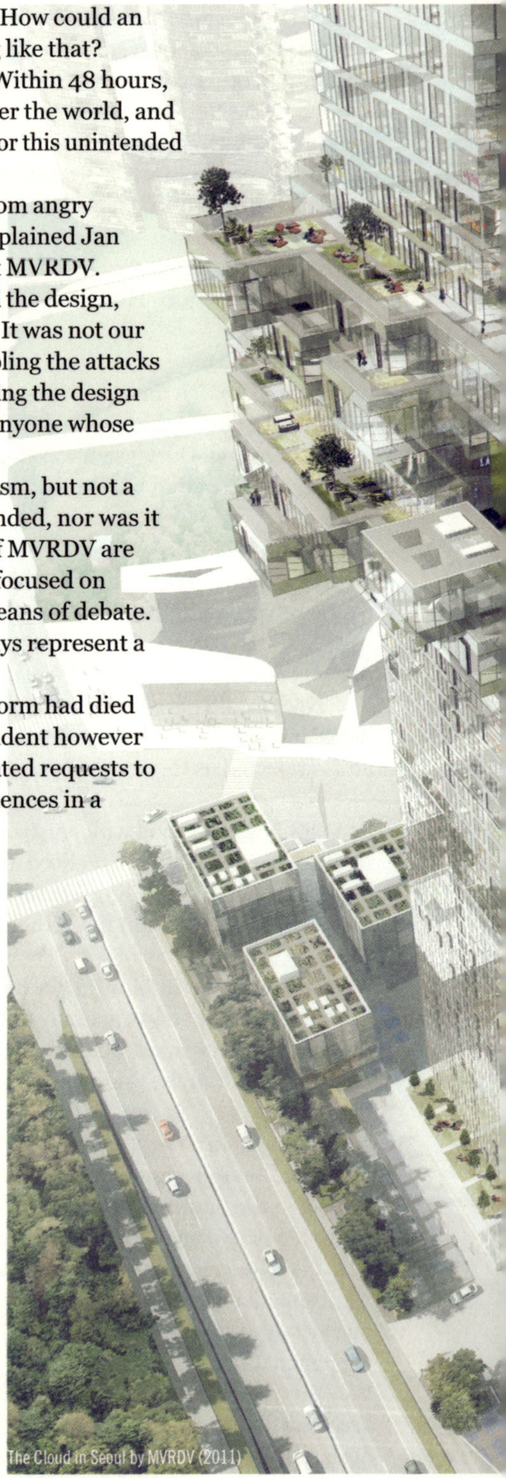

The Cloud in Seoul by MVRDV (2011)

Interview
Bjarke Ingels

'The iconography in our work is always a found object'

Masterplan The Seven Peaks of Azerbaijan on Zira Island in Baku by BIG (2008)

Bjarke Ingels (1974) is a Danish architect. He is a founder of BIG (Bjarke Ingels Group), which has offices in Copenhagen and New York. The book *Yes is More*, published in 2009, takes the form of a comic book in which Bjarke Ingels literally guides the reader through its projects.

BIG recently made a proposal for the renewal of the pier in St. Petersburg, Florida, featuring an explicit iconography. Celebrating life on the waterfront, BIG designed a pier that loops at its end to form a sort of breaking wave. In the words of BIG, the curling deck offers the public 'a surreal moment of bending gravity or warped reality' that is reminiscent of the sensation that a wave offers when curling over you when you're bathing in the sea. BIG has taken a virtue of the beach, scaled it up, and turned it into a theatrical architectural space.

In the design the "wave" offers space for all kinds of activities. BIG proposed including only a leisure program that in some way can be related to the natural cycle of water. Water evaporates, forms clouds and condenses back into rain. Echoing this cycle, one side of the building houses a Turkish bath – representing evaporation – while the highest part of the building holds a "cloud room" with an observation deck. As an extra attraction, at certain times of day rain could fall in the public space that is formed by the warped building.

In BIG's approach, an iconography is never set beforehand. It emerges during the design process from the analysis of the context and the program. In its work, the iconography often broadcasts an abstract idea. That's why the iconography, even though it's quite literally translated into architecture, never becomes banal.

A wonderful example is the Superkilen park that BIG, together with Topotek1 and Superflex, designed in Copenhagen. To celebrate the diversity in the population of that part of the Danish capital, the park is fitted with typical urban furniture from countries all over the world. With such a social-political agenda, this literalness is not banal, but simply a way to communicate the meaning of the park as clearly and directly as possible.

A recurring theme in your work is the building as a landscape. Sometimes these landscapes are more performative, and they allow for walking, cycling or skiing over the building. Sometimes these landscapes are more representational and with their form remind us of hills and mountains. Where does your interest in landscape come from?

'In our projects we aim to create urban spaces. And we want the buildings we design in those projects to behave like good citizens in those urban spaces. If we are to stack spaces anyway, why don't we invite the public to participate? Landscapes allow us to do that. We can turn rooftops and even façades into urban spaces, where all kinds of activities can take place. But we also just don't want to design buildings with boring 2D facades, but aim for a truly 3D urban architecture.'

Bird's-eye view of The Wave in St. Petersburg, USA, by BIG

The Wave in St. Petersburg, USA, by BIG (2011)

Superkilen in Copenhagen by BIG, Topotek1, Superflex, Help Communication and Lemming & Eriksson (2012)

But in some of the projects, like your design for Zira Island in Azerbaijan or the Hurlien Beach Resort in Taiwan, the image of the hills or the mountains is important too.

'In most of the projects the landscapes are purely functional, but it indeed does happen that the image is important too.

An interesting project in this regard is the parking garage with housing on top of it that we designed in Copenhagen. The project has some hill qualities. For the parking garage we had this perforated steel façade that we could turn into a giant artwork, by simply varying the size of the perforations. The client liked the image of the mountain, so we put it up there. We discovered that along the way.

For the same client we designed the master plan for Zira Island, just off the coast of Baku, the capital of Azerbaijan. The municipality was holding back the development of this island. It was afraid it would irreversibly scar the landscape. We designed various towers with various apartment typologies and discovered that we could compare the buildings with the mountains of the country. We would create a landscape that would simultaneously be totally new and look familiar.

Important here is to know that we never start with naming the children. The 8 House housing block in Copenhagen was never designed as an 8. It was designed as a continuous building in which you can walk on different levels. The image in our work, or iconography as you call it, is always a found object.'

A found iconography, as with the master plan for Zira Island, helps you to tie a project to a specific location and to communicate the project to your client and other parties that are involved – like a local government. A very successful project in terms of generating enthusiasm with an iconography was your design of the Ren building for the Expo 2010 in Shanghai. How did this project come about?

'This building was originally designed as a hotel for a site in Sweden. But then one of my Chinese employees recognized the Chinese character for "people" in it. We found that so fascinating that we proposed it for a site in China too. Besides a 1000-room hotel it contained a water sports and conference center.'

You had designed buildings in the form of letters before. Within the master plan for the Danish city of Vejle you proposed to build five apartment buildings that together would spell V-E-J-L-E.

'The municipality of Vejle wanted to connect the city to the water, but simultaneously preserve some of the industrial activities at the harbor. What we therefore proposed was to concentrate the industry on a central pier and envelope this on all sides by parks. The housing that we designed around this area exploits some of the qualities of the harbor. Snaking and cylindrical buildings trace the foundations of former silos.

The buildings that we could design at the waterfront had a particular condition: they would be seen from the high bridge spanning

Scala Tower in Copenhagen by BIG (2007)

The Mountain in Copenhagen by BIG (2007)

8 House in Copenhagen by BIG (2009)

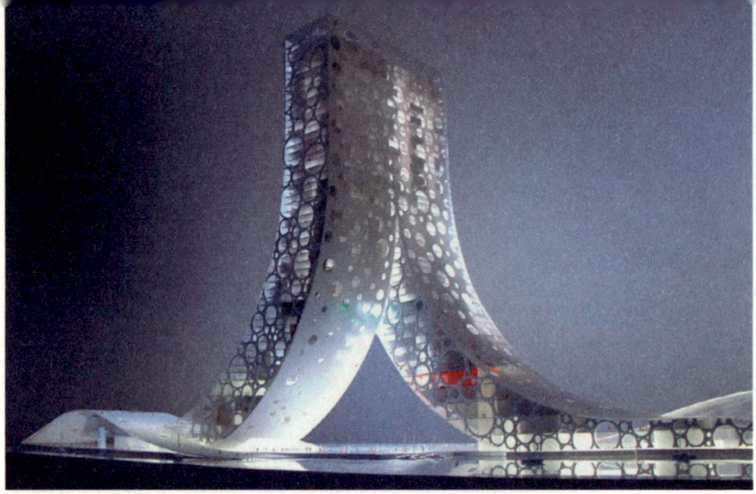

People's Building in Shanghai by BIG and JDS (2004)

Masterplan Vejle Harbour, Denmark, by BIG and JDS (2003)

Arlanda Hotel in Stockholm by BIG (from 2007 onwards)

Walter Tower in Prague by BIG (2007)

The Dunny Show by BIG (2006)

the bay. So we thought we would announce the name of the city to the cars traveling towards it. To create the letters we designed three tower typologies. One typology is repeated – the E – and one typology is mirrored – the L that becomes a J. It is a very appealing scheme with a modern and functional architecture.'

With this iconography you really exploited the potential of the site.

'A somewhat similar project to this is the Arlanda Hotel that we designed for the airport of Stockholm. The charming thing about arriving at this particular airport is that you are introduced to the city by all these pictures of people living there. Our client wanted a box with hotel rooms, so we designed one for him. We just gave the hotel a triangular floor plan so it would have an atrium in the middle. But thinking of these pictures at the airport, we thought it would be nice to add three portraits of the Swedish royal family. We designed panorama windows for the building that would simply contract and expand to form the pixels of the portraits. The building is located where it can be seen from both the air and the highway. And precisely when seen from a distance, the line raster of the façade turns into crystal-clear portraits. It's a serious joke (laughs).'

Could you explain your design for the Walter Tower in Prague? Is the project really to be read as a big W?

'The project had a mix of commercial and residential program. It was also located at the main entrance of a new neighborhood. If we would design the building as a slab, for the neighborhood it would become a wall. We therefore decided to slice up the programmatic volume in such a way that the building below would have the ideal floor plan for the commercial program, but above would have the ideal floor plan for apartments. By twisting the whole volume on ground level, the building is opened towards that neighborhood, while at the floors above the building is opened up towards the sun. This way we could combine the best of connectivity (a slab with big floor plans) and autonomy (towers with small floor plans and a lot of light).'

On your website I found one project without a description: a building in the form of a Dunny Doll children's toy.

'(Laughs) That was some charity work. Some of my friends asked a couple of artists to decorate the Dunny Doll for an exhibition. They asked us too. So we made a Dunny Doll out of floor plates: we made a giant building of it. It would have been a very cool building. At the office we joked that it could be the Dunny Headquarters.'

It is also literally a Duck as Robert Venturi and Denise Scott Brown would describe it.

'If you are interested in ornament, you should definitely look at the Danish Pavilion that we designed for the Expo 2010 in Shanghai.'

I know that project, but never experienced its ornamental side.

'The entire pavilion is basically one big room. You can cycle all the way through it. It also has enormous cantilevers. We therefore designed this giant steel beam running all the way through the building. Engineers very carefully calculated the performance and dimensions of this beam. The stresses that occur in this beam are translated into the perforation pattern of the steel façade. Where the stresses are high the pattern is closed, where the stresses are low the pattern is open. The façade in the end forms a sort of x-ray of the building.'

So this is an ornament that explains the construction! But are people able to understand it without first hearing the story behind it?

'No, I guess not.'

The Greenland National Gallery of Art in Nuuk that BIG has designed takes the form of a perfect circle that is transformed by the topography on which it is projected. This circular plan gives the building a clear organization and flexible exhibition spaces. It also blocks views to the neighborhood behind, while framing views to the sculpture garden and the sea beyond.

The Tamayo Cultural Center that BIG together with Rojkind Architects has designed in Atizapan, Mexico, has the shape of a horizontal cross. This provides the building with a functional organization and equally functional "white box" exhibition spaces. The building is positioned on the sloped site in such a way that it provides a useable shaded space underneath and a roof terrace with a view over Mexico City. BIG calls it 'a symbolic project.'

Many of your designs have a very clear form like a hoop, a circle, an eight, a cross and so on. Is that something you aim for?

'With our architecture we try to achieve a maximum effect with minimal means. We like to concentrate our efforts, to boil it down. We are interested in complexity, but in the way that software engineers regard it. We want to communicate a maximum amount of insight in the most straightforward manner imaginable. We consider complexity as a higher form of simplicity.'

Do these clear forms help also help you in the communication of the project to the client or the public?

'No, they're not meant for that. When we communicate our designs to a client, we just explain what we do and how we do it. That is much easier than to explain exactly how the project uses minimal means to achieve maximum effect. We let the design speak for itself.'

Danish Pavilion on the Shanghai Expo 2010 by BIG (2010)

Greenland National Gallery for Art in Nuuk by BIG (from 2010 onwards)

Tamayo Cultural Center in Atizapan, Mexico, by BIG and Rojkind Architects (2011)

Outroduction

When you ask an architect directly about his/her motivation to use a specific iconography, which I did many times for this book, the answer often begins with 'no, no, no.' It was a question that I could not ask in that way.

The reason for this became clear during the very first interview. A design begins with the brief: the intention of the client, the program of requirements and the physical and cultural context. Like a genuine acrobat, the architect goes to work to find the clearest possible answer to this multifaceted brief. If iconography is used, this is only one of the many elements in the total design. Moreover, it is inseparably linked to the other elements, which it helps to explain. Iconography at the scale of the building – the building as ornament – is inseparably bound to the DNA of the building as a whole. Asking about the iconography of the design is therefore asking about the total design.

The connection between the iconography that is used and the design as a whole forms the basis for the critical framework with which the building as ornament can be assessed. The stronger this connection, the greater the communicative power of the iconography. Only when the iconography is actually rooted in the total design can it truly explain the function, social status, organization, loadbearing structure and/or context of the building.

In some cases, a "thin" iconography – an iconography that is limited to the skin of the building – is sufficient. But the most convincing examples are when a "thick" iconography is used – an iconography that enters into dialogue with each element of the design: its integration into the (urban) landscape, its organization and its loadbearing structure and its interior design. If the chosen iconography has emerged from the total design, then its application throughout the design strengthens the character of the building. As a result, the design will acquire a unique and legible character. The building will become eloquent. The communicative dimension that emanates from iconography provides a much more precise response to the brief than doing without this communication.

A recurring theme in the debate about the use of iconography in architecture is the question: when does it become too flat, when does it degenerate into "Disney"? This question refers to an overly literal translation of the image into architecture. The result is more of an image than a building. A good example is the restaurant in the shape of a duck, which the architects Robert Venturi and Denise Scott Brown encountered in the vicinity of New York City. With the critical framework proposed here, it can be stated that the image of the duck explains the function of the building: it is a restaurant that specializes in duck. The public will probably experience the image of the duck as a virtue, even though the silhouette of the duck is emphasized rather heavily, and other physical characteristics of the animal are negated. Striking though is that the chosen iconography does not emerge from the total design. The entrance does not fit properly into the design, and there is no space for windows. This thin use of iconography turns out to be a flat one.

There is no dialogue whatsoever between the image and the underlying building. While that is the crux. It is the dialogue between the image and the underlying construction that ensures that the building remains a building.

Opinions differ about how literally an image can be translated into architecture. The proponents of a more literal iconography, such as Winy Maas and Bjarke Ingels, praise the clear communication to the public that is achieved with this approach. Others, such as Alejandro Zaero-Polo, Ben van Berkel and Steven Holl, fear that an overly literal iconography will be consumed too easily by the public; to continue to captivate the public during repeated visits to the building, they focus instead on a layered iconography. The risk of the first approach is that the iconography quickly becomes boring; the risk of the second approach is that the iconography is too abstract to be legible. Consequently, both approaches have pros and cons. This also applies to the use of iconography in architectural details, as advocated by Adriaan Geuze and Michiel Riedijk. Due to its small scale, iconographic detail is excellent when experienced at a short distance, but lacks emanation to its surroundings, urban or otherwise.

Regardless of the type of iconography, all the architects interviewed in this book emphasized in their own way that the architecture must never become the actual image. A certain degree of abstraction is always required. The building must remain a building. But how can be determined if an iconography is too literal? The link between iconography and visual arts indicates that the required level of abstraction is highly culture-specific. Consequently, it is dynamic. At different points in time and at different places, different levels of abstraction are required. In the assessment of an iconography personal taste therefore shouldn't be leading. Foremost the cultural context should be considered.

Finding a suitable iconography requires much craftsmanship from the architectural firms. The flood of criticism that MVRDV received when its design for a dual residential tower in Seoul reminded many people of the attacks on the Twin Towers in New York demonstrates convincingly that the use of iconography requires a different architectural approach. In their internal discussions, architectural firms should openly address the representational aspects of their designs. Subsequently, the most powerful metaphors should be tested on a public. Only then can an eloquent public architecture emerge and can be guaranteed that the iconography will be experienced by everyone as a virtue.

Finally, there is the question of whether architects should strive to maximize the architectural means in every design that they make, whether it is for a villa, an apartment house, an office building or a public building. Among the architects interviewed for this book, there is no absolute agreement on this question. For example, both Winy Maas and Bjarke Ingels use housing to make big gestures in the landscape, which is something that Denise Scott Brown and Michiel Riedijk detest. Something can be said in favor of both positions. The strict hierarchy of buildings that existed until the end of the nineteenth century has been replaced by a more open picking order. In addition, the urban landscape at many places in the world has become much more amorphous. This gives architects much more freedom than before.

But even in our current society, there is still a certain hierarchy. To be able to truly explain the function and status of a building, an architect must be aware of this hierarchy. The means available to the architect to explain the character of a building have expanded enormously in the past decades. However, this is no reason to use all of these means all of the time. A building that accommodates a function that is viewed as important in society must show this importance in its architecture. And a building with a more public character should manifest itself more explicitly in the urban landscape than a building with a more private character. This is called propriety. And in this way, the city remains legible.

The critical framework for the use of iconography ultimately looks like this:

- Does the iconography explain the function, social status, organization, load-bearing structure and/or context of the building?
- Does the chosen iconography emerge from the total design, and is the depth of the iconography appropriate to how the design is structured?
- Is the level of abstraction of the iconography compatible with the cultural context of the building?
- Does the public experience the chosen iconography as a virtue?
- Does the degree of expression of the building match its social status and publicness in society and in the urban landscape?

Throughout history, the most diverse images have been used for the ornament, from leaves to half-naked men. In the contemporary ornament, the palette of images used is even richer, ranging from national flags to comic text balloons. As to its themes, in principle everything is possible. Although a new parameter has been introduced with the scaling up of the ornament to the scale of the building as a whole: the chosen image must be compatible with the structure of the building. Images that are essentially based on their outline – such as letters and hills – and images that are based on their volume and texture – such as rocks, waves and sails – are simpler to use in this respect than images whose effect is based on a very precise drawing – such as people and animals. In general terms, construction is about stacking, and images that in themselves are more abstract are more compatible with this than images that in themselves are already extremely literal.

Interesting in this regard is that a design in which part of the iconography is literal, but another part remains more abstract, can appeal directly to the public, but is not assessed as "Disney". The Schaulager Museum in Basel, designed by the Swiss architectural firm Herzog & de Meuron, has a façade which appears to have been pulled up from the ground, with a texture and coloring that echoes a section of the soil. However, the sharply incised building volume at the entrance provides nuance to that iconography. In this way, the whole building remains truly a building.

Of the types of building as ornament mentioned in the Introduction – iconographic detail, layered iconography, singular iconography – the latter appears to be the most widely used in practice, which is due to its communicative power. However, just as much can be said in favor of the more implicit experience that accompanies layered iconography and the different ways iconographic detail is experienced from a distance and from nearby. Every type of iconography works in its own way and can be the best solution for a specific brief.

In the past decades the building as ornament has acquired a reputation of being costly and impractical. Indeed, it was often expensive, but it will not remain so. The communicative power emanated by the building as ornament is finding its way, slowly but surely, to the broader production of buildings.

Totally new products are often accessible only by the wealthy. This applied to the first automobiles, but also to the first Modernistic homes. Nothing was as expensive as modern living, in any case during the 1920s and 1930s. Several decades later, the building industry had made its transition, and modern living became accessible to everyone.

The same is now happening with the use of iconography in architecture. The Guggenheim Museum in Bilbao, the Yokohama International Port Terminal and the Bird's Nest Stadium in Beijing are all very expensive buildings. Even though these buildings were designed with the latest software, in many cases the construction itself still required traditional, manual labor. But in the meantime, the building industry is innovating. Freeform buildings can be produced more and more easily with computer-controlled manufacturing. The high costs that gave the first generation of iconographic buildings its bad reputation will decline significantly with the second generation of these buildings.

This development is happening in parallel with the rapid dissemination of this architectural approach and the advantages that it offers. Whereas up to the end of the twentieth century only a few pioneers experimented with it, in the present century a much larger group of architects has started working with it. With the undiminished high demand for a more specific and eloquent architecture, this group of architects is bound to grow further in the future.

Iconography is seen by various architecture critics as an outgrowth of capitalism. The commercial success that the multinational Guggenheim Museum achieved with it in Bilbao, and the subsequent quest by cities all over the world to reproduce the Bilbao effect, is the cause of this criticism. But it must not be forgotten that iconography is only an architectural means. As such, it can be used for everything. Iconography can put a city on the map internationally, but it can just as well bring attention to a new neighborhood facility. An example of the latter is the new public library designed by Giancarlo Mazzanti in the second city of Colombia. The rock iconography emphasizes that this building is a long-term investment in the neighborhood. The solidity of the rock evokes confidence in the permanence of this new facility.

Whereas the primary intention of the first generation of iconographic buildings was to attract as much attention as possible (quantitative communication), the second generation has a much more nuanced message (qualitative communication). This is only partly the result of the financial crisis that held the Western world in its grasp for several years after 2008. More important is that the iconographic building has matured. The messages told by these buildings are becoming increasingly diverse, more precise and more deeply rooted in society. Local culture, emancipation and sustainability – these are themes that will delineate the building as ornament in the years to come.

Illustration Credits

a = above
m = middle
b = below
l = left
r = right

Projects
Inside front cover – p.1: Mikkel Frost
p.2: Cino Zucchi
p.3: Adam Mörk
p.4 – p.5: Patricia Parinejad
p.6a: Nigel Young
p.6b – p.7b: 3XN
p.8a: Gareth Gardner
p.8b – p.9b: Hufton+Crow
p.10 – p.11: Snøhetta
p.12: Maggi Moreno
p.13: Nigel Young
p.14: Magma architecture
p.15: Ben McMillan
p.16 – p.17: Philipp Shaerer

Introduction
p.26 – p.27, p.41m, p.42: Iwan Baan
p.29: Jeroen Musch
p.30a, p.30bl, p.30br: Claude-Nicolas Ledoux
p.31: Jean-Antoine Alavoine
p.32: Johann David Steingruber
p.32: Moonik/Wikipedia
p.34: Iñigo Alkorta/Flickr
p.35: Floyd B. Bariscale/Flickr
p.36: Luis Sandoval Mandujano/iStockphoto
p.39al: Nigel Young
p.39ar: SWFC
p.39m: MVRDV
p.39b: Georges Fessy
p.41b: Satoru Mishima
p.45a: Luxigon
p.45b: Arup

Interview Auke van der Woud
p.46 – p.47, p.51a, p.51b, p.52a: Stadsarchief Amsterdam
p.52b: Rob 't Hart
p.54 – p.55: Jan Leliman

Interview Denise Scott Brown
p.58 – p.59, p.63a, p.63m, p.65, p.66al, p.66ar, p.66m, p.66b, p.69a, p.69b, p.71a, p.71m, p.71b, p.72a, p.72b – p.73b: VSBA
p.61: Roel Backaert

Interview Charles Jencks
p.76 – p.77: Michel Denancé
p.79l, p.79r, p.84: Charles Jencks
p.80a: RSH+P
p.80m: Morley von Sternberg
p.80b: Jim Gourley
p.82a, p.82b: Nigel Young
p.82m, p.86a: Iwan Baan
p.86m: Bitter Bredt
p.86b: Elliot Lewis
p.87: Scott Francis
p.89a: Manuel Gonzalez Vicente
p.89m: Foster + Partners
p.89b: OMA

Collage Alphabet
p.90 – p.91: JDS
p.92: Ruijing Photo
p.93a, p.94a: BIG
p.93b, p.94a – p.95a: BIG and JDS
p.94b: NL Architects
p.95b: Bay Arch
p.96a: Steven Holl Architects
p.96b – p.97bl: Waterstudio.NL
p.97a: MVRDV
p.97bl: Ivo Wennekes

Interview Adriaan Geuze
p.98 – p.99, p.100m, p.100b – p.101b, p.102m – p.103m, p.102b, p.105m, p.105bl, p.105br, p.107a, p.107b, p.108, p.109, p.110, p.112m, p.112b, p.113: West 8
p.112a: Jeroen Musch

Interview Michiel Riedijk
p.114 – p.115, p.119a, p.122m, p.122b: Jeroen Musch
p.117a, p.117b, p.125a, p.125b, p.128, p.129: Daria Scagliola/Stijn Brakkee
p.117m: Jan Kempenaers
p.119b: Wally Gobetz
p.122a: Sarah Blee

Interview Alejandro Zaero-Polo
p.130 – p.131, p.134al, p.134ar, p.134b: Satoru Mishima
p.132: Valerie Bennett
p.137a: Francisco Andeyro García
p.137ml, p.137bl, p.138m, p.138b, p.139m, p.141m, p.143: Foreign Office Architects
p.137mr: Cristobal Palma
p.137br: Jordi Todo
p.141a: Benedict Luxmoore
p.141b: Alvaro Arroyo/iStockphoto
p.142: United Architects

Interview Ben van Berkel
p.144 – p.145, p.149m, p.149b, p.150b, p.153ml, p.153b, p.154al, p.154ar, p.154ml, p.154mr, p.154b: Christian Richters
p.147a, p.147m, p.147b, p.148: United Architects
p.150a, p.152, p.156b – p.157b, p.157m: UNStudio
p.153a, p.153mr: Iwan Baan

Collage Islands
p.158 – p.159: NASA
p.160b, p.161b: Nakheel
p.161a: (designed by) Erick van Egeraat
p:162: Innovatieplatform
p.162a: Noor
p.163b: West 8
p.164a: Waterstudio.NL
p.164b: De Jong Luchtfotografie
p.165: BIG and JDS

Interview Steven Holl
p.166 – p.167, p.169, p.171bl, p.171br, p.173a, p.173m, p.173b: Iwan Baan
p.168ml, p.171a, p.175m, p.178a, p.178ml: Steven Holl Architects
p.168mr, p.175a, p.176a, p.176m, p.176b, p.179a, p.179b: Paul Werchol
p.170, p.178mr, p.178b: Andy Ryan
p.175b: Simon Woolley/iStockphoto

Interview Winy Maas
p.180 – p.181, p.182 – p.183, p.185a, p.187b, p.192m, p.192b, p.194a, p.194b – p.195b, p.198 – p.199: MVRDV
p.185m, p.185b: Luxigon
p.187a, p.188m: Philippe Ruault
p.188a, p.188b, p.197: Rob 't Hart
p.190, p.191: Jeroen Musch

Interview Bjarke Ingels
p.200 – p.201, p.203a, p.203m, p.205a, p.206mr, p.206bl, p.206br, p.209m, p.209b: BIG
p.203b, p.209a: Iwan Baan
p.205m: Jens Lindhe
p.205b: Dragor Luftfoto
p.206a, p.206ml: BIG and JDS

Projects
p.220 – p.221: Sergio Gómez
p.222 – p.223: Ruedi Walti
p.224, p.239: Christian Richters
p.225: Margherita Spiluttini
p.226 – p.227: Arup
p.228b – p.229b: MAD
p.229: 24H > architecture
p.230a: Tjep.
p.230b – p.231b: Siemens
p.232 – p.233: Iwan Baan
p.234 – p.235: Herzog & de Meuron
p.236: **Philippe Ruault**
p.237: Gerrit Schreurs
p.238: FR-EE
p.240 – inside back cover: Burj Al Arab

About the Author

Michiel van Raaij (1980) was trained as an architect at Delft University of Technology (TU Delft). During his study he already devoted much of his time to research and publications. Van Raaij was, for example, involved in the organization of the *Projective Landscape Conference* and the publication that coincided with it. For a term of one year he was editor-in-chief of the students' architecture magazine *Pantheon//*. Van Raaij was also project leader of the collection of short stories by students *Het Nieuwe Lijden* (The New Suffering) that came about in collaboration with guest writer Arnon Grunberg.

Based on his fascination with the growing use of iconography in contemporary architecture, from 2006 to 2010 Van Raaij published a successful blog – *Eikongraphia* – in which he mapped out the phenomenon. This blog became the prelude to this book.

After graduating, Michiel van Raaij began working at *Architectenweb*, a leading architecture platform in the Netherlands. Since 2010 he has been editor-in-chief of *Architectenweb*. In this position, he not only directs the editorial team and network of *Architectenweb.nl* and *Architectenweb magazine*, but he also organizes numerous events – from network breakfasts to conferences.

LinkedIn: nl.linkedin.com/in/michielvanraaij
Twitter: @michielvanraaij
E-mail: michielvanraaij@gmail.com

Acknowlegements

I would like to thank all interviewed historians and architects as well as their firms. Also thanks to Bernard Colenbrander, Otakar Máčel, Geoff Manaugh, Marieken Oostrom, Selma van der Meijs, my parents, the team at Architectenweb and all my friends.

Credits

Texts: Michiel van Raaij
Copy editing: Bookmakers, Nijmegen
Translation: Charles Frink / Bookmakers
Design: Joseph Plateau grafisch ontwerpers, Amsterdam
Lithography and printing: Van Gorcum BV
Publisher: Marcel Witvoet, nai010 publishers

nai010 publishers is an internationally orientated publisher specialized in developing, producing and distributing books in the fields of architecture, urbanism, art and design. www.nai010.com

nai010 books are available internationally at selected bookstores and from the following distribution partners:

North, Central and South America - Artbook | D.A.P., New York, USA, dap@dapinc.com

Germany, Austria, Italy, Spain, Portugal and Greece - Coen Sligting Bookimport, Alkmaar, the Netherlands, sligting@xs4all.nl

Rest of the world - Idea Books, Amsterdam, the Netherlands, idea@ideabooks.nl

For general questions, please contact nai010 publishers directly at sales@nai010.com or visit our website www.nai010.com for further information.

Printed and bound in the Netherlands
ISBN 978-94-6208-044-7

Also available as ebook edition:
Building as Ornament epub
ISBN 978-94-6208-077-5

Projects

España Library Park in Medellín, Colombia by Giancarlo Mazzanti (2005-2007)

To better connect some of the informal settlements within the second city of Colombia, a network of cableways has been constructed. One of these cableways leads to a hill on which this library has been built. In order to give this public investment the most robust expression possible, Giancarlo Mazzanti designed the building as an ensemble of rocks.

Schaulager in Basel by Herzog & de Meuron (1998-2003)

The Schaulager does not just look as if it literally has been pulled from the ground, this is actually the case: the pebbles that were excavated during construction of the building have been used in the façade. In the Schaulager art is stored under the best conditions possible. In the view of Herzog & de Meuron, the permanence of the art that is stored here is best expressed in the metaphor of the earth. What is more stable than that?

Erick van Egeraat Office Tower in Amsterdam by (designed by) Erick van Egeraat (2002-2009)

As the result of the necessary load-bearing structure, office towers often have a somewhat heavier basis and get more immaterial towards their top. In this office tower on the South axis of Amsterdam Erick van Egeraat has turned this scheme upside down. Since the building is located between other towers, the challenge was to get as much daylight as possible into the lower part of the building. Meanwhile, the façade higher up in the building could remain more closed. From his fascination for the beauty hidden in nature, Erick van Egeraat chose to design the building as an elevated rock formation on a fully glazed basis.

To control the lights, switches, et cetera on a marshaling yard in Basel this six-story machine building has been realized. To express its function Herzog & de Meuron has wrapped the building in 20 cm wide copper strips, which have been twisted at certain places to allow daylight in. The copper skin functions as a cage of Faraday, thus protecting the installations from radiation outside. As a whole the building looks like an abstracted spool. Its copper skin provides the building with a certain scalelessness, which has allowed the building to become an integral part of the technical railway landscape.

Signal Box in Basel by Herzog & de Meuron (1989-1994)

When water is heavily disturbed, bubbles inevitably emerge. The lightweight roof structure of the Watercube is not only a very efficient cover for the Olympic swimming pools in Beijing, but also symbolizes well the battle inside between man and water. The seemingly arbitrariness of the façade pattern gives the Watercube a particular resemblance to the neighboring Bird's Nest Stadium.

Watercube in Beijing by PTW Architects and Arup (2008)

One World One Dream

In many of its designs MAD aims to eliminate the difference between nature and the built environment. In this 800-meter long residential complex at the Chinese coast the office succeeded in this. Instead of an ensemble of buildings, it has become a landscape attraction; including peaks with viewpoints, terraced gardens, picturesque vistas and dramatic drops.

As if a couple of large Eucalyptus leaves just happened to have fallen on this hill; that is how 24H > architecture describes its design for this villa on Corsica. By giving the wings of the building elongated, oval forms, they can be carefully fitted onto this steep, irregularly formed slope. Especially in the lower parts of Corsica lots of Eucalyptus trees are found; by referring to this the villa is firmly anchored in the natural landscape of the island.

Fake Hills in Beihei, China, by MAD (2008-2014)

Villa Sperone on Corsica by 24H > architecture (2014)

Lucky Building in New York by Tjep. (2010)

Fascinated by the principle of pixilation Tjep. developed a vase in which the image of a laughing child was hidden. According to Tjep. the same principle can be applied to an architectural scale: 'Who would want to crash a plane into such a friendly looking building?'

On the north bank of the river Thames, opposite the O2 Arena, Siemens has built a center where it wants to further develop its knowledge about sustainability and share this with the public. To underline this mission the building itself has been fitted with all kinds of equipment, allowing it to use as little base materials as possible. According to Wilkinson Eyre the faceted form of the building is an answer to the architecture of the O2 Arena. The name of the building is derived from its faceted form.

Siemens Urban Sustainability Centre, The Crystal, in London by Wilkinson Eyre (2010-2012)

Most of the time, the auditorium of the progressive Jewish congregation in Amsterdam is only used by small groups. During the holidays however, it has to accommodate up to 800 people. To keep the auditorium intimate for small groups, SeARCH chose to limit the floor plan and extend the space vertically with no less than four balconies. The usual layout of the auditorium, with parallel benches facing each other, in combination with these balconies resulted in a façadc that, when lit from the inside at night, represents the burning bush that Moses found on Mount Sinai and its representation in Jewism: the Menorah chandelier.

LJG Synagogue in Amsterdam by SeARCH (2005-2010)

Elbphilharmonie in Hamburg by Herzog & de Meuron (2003-2016)

At the site of its old port, Hamburg is building a new city quarter: Hafencity. This development is crowned by the new concert hall, which has a hotel wrapped around it, that is positioned on top of the old Kaispeicher A warehouse. With its undulating roofline and bubbling glass façade the Elbphilharmonie looks a bit like a raised block of water. Since Hamburg, as a port city, relies heavily on the water, a more virtuous iconography seems hardly possible.

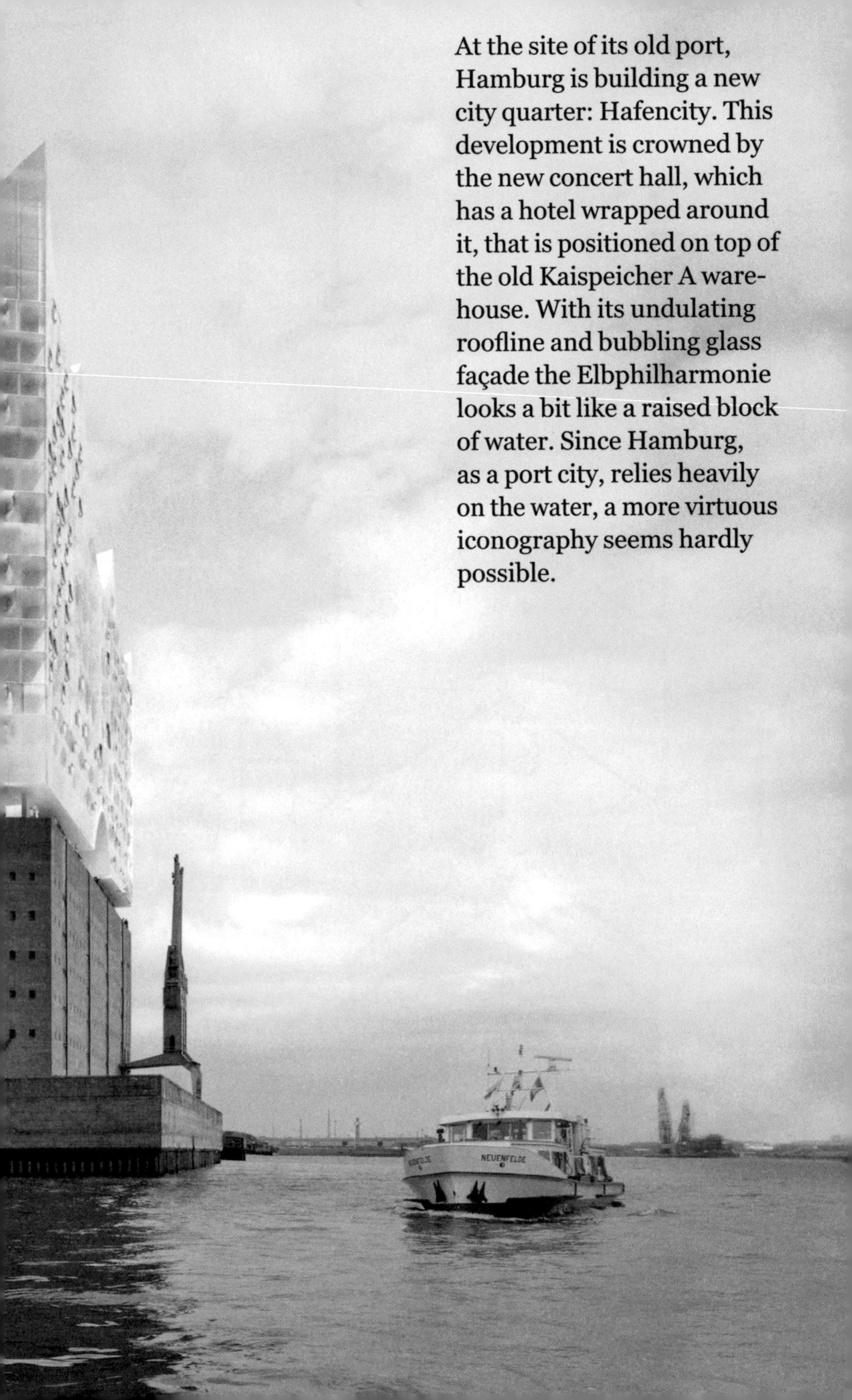

Citroën Flagship Showroom in Paris by Manuelle Gautrand (2002-2007)

Would first-time visitors notice it? Or would they only recognize it after a while? Between the flat glass façade at ground level and the free formed glass façade above, Manuelle Gautrand has subtly introduced two chevrons: the logo of the Citroën automobiles that are shown here on Champs Elysées.

In the city center of The Hague, Archipelontwerpers has renovated a series of buildings and designed new houses above the shops there. At the end of the nineteenth century, on one of the corners of this building block stood an organically shaped building. With this new construction the architecture office brought back the essence of that building in a contemporary way.

The Gown in The Hague by Archipelontwerpers (2005)

After the apparition of the Virgin Mary in Mexico City in 1531, the first Catholic Church was built there. For the Catholic community in Miami FR-EE has designed a new church in honor of Our Lady of Guadalupe, as she was called. In its design the architecture office decided to include extra bays for all of the 27 virgins of South-America. Extrusion of all these bays resulted in this corrugated building volume, which according to FR-EE refers to Mary's pleated cloak.

Chapel in Miami by FR-EE (from 2012 onwards)

HydraPier in Hoofddorp, the Netherlands, by Asymptote (2002)

For the Floriade international flower and gardening exhibition, Asymptote designed a pavilion representing the surrounding area, the Haarlemmermeer polder. Due to the presence of Schiphol international airport, airplanes are always visible above this reclaimed land. The architecture office translated this duality into the architecture of the pavilion. The tilted and streamlined steel volume, with cantilevers like wings, points to aviation explicitly. The water that permanently cascades between the lower building parts acknowledges life under sea level in a slightly more abstract way.

The only 7-star hotel in the world, as the Burj Al Arab sometimes is called, stands on its own little island off the coast of Dubai. In its design Atkins incorporated elements of the dhow, a small Arab ship. The atrium that runs over the entire height of the building is fitted with an enormous convex synthetic canvas. The hotel rooms are organized on V-shaped floors that are anchored by a 322-meter high mast.

Burj Al Arab in Dubai by Atkins (1993-1999)